The Theory of Constraints and Its Implications for Management Accounting

by

Eric Noreen, Ph.D., CMA

Debra Smith, CPA

James T. Mackey, Ph.D., CMA, CPA

A research project sponsored by
The IMA Foundation for Applied Research, Inc.
Research affiliate of the Institute of Management Accountants
Montvale, New Jersey
Price Waterhouse
Paris, France

The North River Press

The IMA Foundation for Applied Research, Inc.
10 Paragon Drive
Montvale, NJ 07645-1760

The IMA Foundation for Applied Research, Inc. is the research affiliate of
the Institute of Management Accountants. The basic purpose of the
Foundation is to develop and disseminate timely management accounting
research findings that can be applied to current and emerging business
issues.

Clare Barth, editor

Published by
The North River Press Publishing Corporation
P.O. Box 567
Great Barrington, MA 01230
(800) 486-2665

Manufactured in the United States of America

IMA Publication Number 95300
ISBN 0-88427-116-1

Foreword_____

The IMA Foundation for Applied Research, Inc. invited Eli Goldratt, originator of the Theory of Constraints, to prepare a foreword for this study. We appreciate his willingness to do so, although the views expressed are strictly his own.

In 1978 I switched from research in physics to researching industry. Almost from the start I was baffled by the use of efficiencies and product cost as performance measurements. It seemed as if industry was using measurements that worked against the stated goal of industry—to make a profit.

As time and my research progressed I became more and more frustrated with the devastating ramifications of the way cost accounting was (and still is) used by managers. Finally, toward the end of 1983, I decided, against all advice, to address the issue in my public lectures. I titled my presentation "Cost Accounting—Public Enemy Number One of Productivity." To my astonishment it was extremely well received by the accounting profession, so much so that I was invited to be a keynote speaker at the 1985 annual conference of the National Association of Accountants (now the Institute of Management Accountants). It turned out that the accounting professionals were aware of, and agreed with, most of the points I had raised. They were even aware of most of my suggested solutions.

That left me with bigger puzzles. If the accounting profession is aware of and agreeable to my criticism and the suggested solutions, how come cost accounting is almost totally ingrained in industry? How come textbooks in accounting do not vigorously condemn it?

Even now I don't have satisfactory answers, but here are some speculations:

- Maybe it is because the nomenclature is obscure—the word "cost" is used for everything. It is used for investment (the cost of a machine); it is used for operating expense (the cost of running a department); it is used for disguising expenses as investments (absorption cost). It is even used for throughput issues that have nothing to do with cost (opportunity cost). Combine these confusing terms with variable cost (which for many companies is quite constant over years), fixed cost (which changes much more over the same number of years), and above all with the most misleading concept, product cost, and you see how modest warnings to do one thing and not another can be understood only by experts.

- Maybe it is because even the persons who understand why the current way of allocating cost to products is leading to erroneous decisions—even they are captured in the general myth of the need for product cost. Otherwise I cannot possibly understand how a "solution" such as activity-based costing was proposed to cure the illness of current accounting systems.

- Maybe it is because the conceptual difference between thinking cost and thinking throughput is not understood. Thinking cost allows (sometimes even forces) a manager to think locally—a work center in isolation, a product in isolation. Thinking throughput forces a manager to think globally.

I don't know.

What I do know is that studies such as this one will help bring the field back to common sense. This monograph is well thought out, logical, and objective and conveys its data and conclusions in a well-paced, interesting style. I wish that all future monographs would be at the level of this one.

Eliyahu M. Goldratt
Kfar-Saba, Israel
January 1995

Introduction _____

Take the laws of physics, add the human element, wrap the culture of the organization around them, and you have an inkling of the approaches advocated by Eli Goldratt and his legion of Jonah followers.[1]

The philosophy of Goldratt's Theory of Constraints (TOC) is well articulated in the literature.[2] What we don't know is how well TOC has been applied in practice (apart from a few isolated instances reported in the literature).What problems are encountered in practice? What success stories are there to tell?

IMA's Foundation for Applied Research presents the first in-depth evaluation ever of TOC, based on investigations at 21 U.S. and European companies. In addition, this report provides tantalizing glimpses of an intriguing new development in the Theory of Constraints. This new development, called the Thinking Process, is no less than an attempt to bring systematic logic to bear on fundamental organizational problems.

Guidance in the preparation of this report was generously provided by the Foundation's Project Committee:

Robert C. Miller
Chairman
The Boeing Company
Seattle, Washington

Otto B. Martinson, CMA
Old Dominion University
Norfolk, Virginia

---

[1] See "Thinking Revolutionary," *Success,* February 1995, pp. 40-48.
[2] See John A. Caspari, "Theory of Constraints," Chapter 8A in *Management Accountants' Handbook*, fourth edition, 1994 Comulative Supplement, Donald E. Keller, James Bulloch, and Robert L. Shultis, eds., New York, John Wiley & Sons, Inc., 1994.

Kenneth Merchant
University of
Southern California
Los Angeles, California

Henry Davis, CMA
Reliance Electric Company
Greenville, South Carolina

This report reflects the views of the researcher and not necessarily those of the trustees for The IMA Foundation for Applied Research, Inc., the IMA, the Committee on Research (which initiated the project), or the Project Committee.

Julian M. Freedman, CMA, CPA, CPIM
Director of Research
Institute of Management Accountants

Acknowledgments

First and foremost, we would like to thank managers at the 21 different companies we visited for their time, hospitality, and willingness to share information freely with us. Without their cooperation, this study would have been impossible.

We would like to thank the Institute of Management Accountants for sponsoring this project. Price Waterhouse also provided crucial funding through its support of the Price Waterhouse Professor of Management Information and Control at INSEAD, the European Institute of Business Administration.

Finally, we would like to thank Eliyahu M. Goldratt for his cooperation throughout this project. He was always willing and eager to exchange ideas and even to serve as a tutor when the need arose.

About the Authors

Eric Noreen, Ph.D., CMA

Eric Noreen has been a member of the University of Washington business school faculty since 1977 and is a Price Waterhouse Professor of Management Information and Control at INSEAD, the European Institute of Business Administration in Fontainebleau, France.

Dr. Noreen's research has appeared in all of the major research journals in accounting. Most recently, his research has centered on fundamental issues in management accounting such as the assumptions underlying cost accounting models and studies of the actual behavior of costs in organizations. Dr. Noreen is the author of *Computer-Intensive Methods for Testing Hypotheses* and is coauthor with Dr. Ray Garrison of the Seventh Edition of *Management Accounting*, the best-selling introductory textbook in management accounting. He is an associate editor of the *Journal of Accounting and Economics* and is on the editorial board of the *Journal of Management Accounting Research* and the *Accounting Review.*

Dr. Noreen is a 1968 Phi Beta Kappa graduate of the University of Washington in mathematics and economics and served as an officer in the U.S. Navy during the Vietnam conflict. He earned both of his advanced business degrees at Stanford University—an MBA in 1974 and a Ph.D. in 1977. He is a Certified Management Accountant.

Debra A. Smith, CPA

Debra Smith is a professor of accounting in the School of Business and Public Administration at the University of Puget Sound in Tacoma, Washington. She received her undergraduate degree in accounting and economics at the University of Idaho, is a graduate of the University of Washington's Executive MBA program, and is a Certified Public Accountant in the state of Washington.

Prior to teaching, Professor Smith worked in public accounting for Touche, Ross & Company, now Deloitte, Touche, and spent nine years in publicly traded manufacturing firms both as a division controller and a vice president of finance and operations. Her research has focused on understanding the changes necessary in measurement and accounting systems to support continuous improvement processes in manufacturing. She is an academic associate of the Goldratt Institute and lectures widely on the Theory of Constraints (TOC) and accounting. She currently is involved in offering workshops explaining the necessary changes in measurement and accounting systems to support quality improvement processes such as just-in-time (JIT), total quality management (TQM), and the Theory of Constraints.

James T. Mackey, Ph.D., CMA, CPA

Jim Mackey has served as a professor of cost and managerial accounting in the School of Business at California State University-Sacramento since 1987. Before assuming this position, he taught in the graduate programs of the University of Wisconsin-Madison, the University of Michigan-Ann Arbor, and York University in Canada.

A frequent contributor to *Management Accounting*, Dr. Mackey also has published in the *Journal of Management Accounting Research*, *CMA Magazine*, *Advances in Accounting*, *Information and Management*, and other journals. He was responsible for editing and writing the

IMA's cases on the Theory of Constraints, published as *Cases from Management Accounting Practice*, Volume 8. For the past 15 years his research interests have centered on the use of accounting systems in manufacturing settings. He often gives seminars and consults on the changes to accounting systems necessitated by new technologies.

Dr. Mackey graduated from the University of Illinois in 1981 with a Ph.D. in accountancy. He also completed a minor area in industrial engineering. His undergraduate degree is in economics and mathematics from the University of Guelph in Canada. It was followed by an MBA in accounting and finance from McMaster University in Canada. His professional designations include CMA and CPA. He is also an academic associate of the Goldratt Institute.

Table of Contents_____

Exhibits_____

Executive Summary_____

The core idea in the Theory of Constraints (TOC) is that every real system such as a profit-making enterprise must have at least one constraint. If it were not true, then the system would produce an infinite amount of whatever it strives for. In the case of a profit-making enterprise, it would be infinite profits. Because a constraint is a factor that limits the system from getting more of whatever it strives for, then a business manager who wants more profits must manage constraints. There really is no choice in this matter. Either you manage constraints or they manage you. The constraints will determine the output of the system whether they are acknowledged and managed or not.

Most businesses can be viewed as a linked sequence of processes that transform inputs into saleable outputs. In TOC, an analogy often is drawn between such a system and a chain. If you want to improve the strength of a chain, what is the most effective way to do it? Do you concentrate on strengthening the strongest link? Do you concentrate on strengthening the largest link? Do you apply efforts uniformly over all the links? Or should you attempt to identify the weakest link and then concentrate efforts on strengthening that single link? Clearly, the last course will bring the biggest benefit in relation to the effort expended.

Continuing with this analogy, the procedure to follow in strengthening the chain is straightforward.

■ First, identify the weakest link, which is the constraint. Identifying it may not be easy because most business processes attempt to cope with fluctuating demands and random disruptions by maintaining buffer inventories at each step of the process. These work-in-process inventories hide problems, obscure interdependencies, and make it difficult to identify the real constraint in the system.

■ Second, don't try to subject the system to too great a load. If a larger load is placed on the chain than the weakest link can handle, the chain will break. The weakest link should set the pace for the entire system.

■ Third, concentrate improvement efforts on the weakest link.

■ Fourth, if the improvement efforts are successful, eventually the weakest link will improve to the point where it is no longer the weakest link. Any further efforts to improve the former weakest link will provide little or no benefit. At this point, the new weakest link must be identified, and the improvement efforts must be shifted over to that link.

This sequential process focuses resources where they will do the most good and is a basic blueprint for continuous improvement. The TOC approach to continuous improvement is a perfect complement to total quality management (TQM)—focusing TQM efforts with laser-like precision on the point in the system where they are likely to be most effective. Unfortunately, we did not observe this blending of TOC and TQM at the sites we visited simply because very few were involved in TQM in any major way. For the most part, managers at TOC sites did not feel the need to get involved in another program because they were pleased with the results just from using the tools available in TOC.

The Theory of Constraints comprises two major groups of techniques—methods for dealing with physical production constraints on the one hand and generic, problem-solving tools on the other.

The generic, problem-solving tools evolved *after* the methods for dealing with physical production constraints were developed. The reasons for this evolution provide some insights into what TOC is all about. Eli Goldratt first became interested in business because of the shop scheduling problem, but he quickly realized that simply improving scheduling would have limited benefits. Further, sustained improvement within a production facility would depend on how the constraints of the process were managed. His first book, *The Goal,* was the product of this thinking and is concerned almost entirely with managing production constraints. The techniques illustrated in *The Goal,* such as Drum-Buffer-Rope scheduling and the five steps for continuous improvement by focusing on the constraints, can be applied quickly and easily to capacity-constrained job shops with high product diversity. Applying these techniques almost always results in immediate payoffs in terms of greater throughput, improved due date performance, and reduced cycle times. We found this payoff to be the case in nearly all of the companies we visited.

Unfortunately, there are limitations to this focus on job shop bottlenecks. Because of the way *The Goal* was written, TOC has been pigeonholed largely as "a manufacturing thing" relevant only in a job shop that is having difficulty meeting due dates. This impression is incorrect—TOC is actually much broader, but most people have difficulty seeing the connections to other situations. Nevertheless, the perception that TOC is applicable only to capacity-constrained job shops has led to difficulties.

Because of the recession, in recent years production bottlenecks did not seem to be a major problem in many companies. And even in companies where the constraint *was* a production bottleneck, production managers who effectively implemented ideas from *The Goal* usually found that the constraint eventually shifted outside of the factory. At that point, further improvement would often be stymied because managers outside of production did not see the relevance of TOC. And once improvement ceases, morale may suffer and the organization may regress. This situation is one of the potential pit-falls of improperly implementing TOC that any potential adopter should be aware of.

These difficulties led to the development of a generic approach for diagnosing and solving problems called the "Thinking Process." According to the claims made by TOC advocates, this approach can be used to solve virtually any problem anywhere in an organization. Viewed from a broader perspective, the principles laid out in *The Goal* for managing a shop are simply examples of the application of the Thinking Process to a particular set of problems. Using the Thinking Process, TOC would no longer be confined inappropriately to the shop floor. The generic Thinking Process approach involves building logical "trees," which basically are cause-and-effect diagrams. Starting with observed symptoms of problems, cause-and-effect reasoning is used to deduce underlying causes, or core problems. This process is very similar to medical diagnosis, which also starts with observed symptoms from which an underlying cause is deduced. Other logical trees then are used to identify and refine solutions. Details of the Thinking Process are sketched in the Appendix. From a theoretical standpoint, the Thinking Process appears to be a remarkably coherent and complete system for logical problem solving that probably would be endorsed by Star Trek's Mr. Spock. Not surprisingly, it is complex and difficult to master and is still being refined.

In general, at the sites we visited managers were dissatisfied with how much of the Theory of Constraints they had put into practice. They were happy with what they had done but usually felt that they should have done more and were hampered by lack of time or lack of confidence and skills. This view was particularly true in regard to the Thinking Process: we found very few managers who were using these tools on a routine basis, although a few were. However, we hasten to add that it may simply be too early to fairly assess the usefulness of the Thinking Process. This complex set of tools is very new, and few of the managers we interviewed had been fully trained in its use. We believe this tool is potentially extraordinarily powerful and flexible, and it has been used quite successfully at a few sites. So despite the generally disappointing results, we suggest that you take the time to familiarize yourself with the Thinking Process as discussed briefly in Chapter 2 and more thoroughly in the Appendix.

Leaving aside the use of the Thinking Process, about half the sites we visited were running their operations almost exclusively using the TOC approach outlined in *The Goal.* The others were using some TOC principles but were attempting to run their operations using other, often inconsistent, approaches as well. Those who were consistently using the TOC approach seemed to be much more satisfied with their operations and to have fewer problems.

Companies that used TOC consistently generally reported impressive gains in financial results and in key operating statistics such as cycle time and due date performance. As often stated in the TQM and JIT literature as well, the success of any program that involves a major cultural change in an organization depends critically on the involvement of top management. At sites where top management did not view the business from a TOC perspective, there were usually—but not always—problems. The biggest problems were with top managers who continued to evaluate production managers based on measures of efficiency rather than profit.

It is impossible to disentangle TOC operations from TOC accounting. Any attempt to run a TOC operation while using traditional management accounting measures and controls is doomed to failure. Like TQM and JIT, TOC is inconsistent with common management accounting practices such as absorption costing and standard cost variance reporting. The biggest single reason for this incompatibility is that both absorption costing and standard variance reporting create incentives to produce excess inventories. Under absorption costing, building up inventories tends to reduce the apparent average cost of goods sold. When production exceeds sales, fixed costs are spread across more units, and some of the fixed costs are reported on the balance sheet as part of additional inventories rather than on the income statement as part of cost of goods sold. Under standard cost variance reporting, a work center with a fixed labor force can improve its efficiency measure only by producing more output. By definition, the nonconstraint work centers can produce output faster than the constraint work centers can. Therefore, if the nonconstraint work centers are kept busy producing output to generate favorable efficiency reports, the inevitable result is a buildup of excessive work-in-process inventories that cannot be turned into salable output. The central message of JIT is that such work-in-process inventories are the cause of major operating problems and tend to camouflage problems that should be dealt with.

Instead of absorption costing, most TOC companies use a variation of variable costing in which it is assumed that direct materials are the only variable cost. Variable costing is preferred to absorption costing under TOC for three reasons:

- ■ It does not create incentives to build up inventories;
- ■ It is considered more useful in decisions; and
- ■ It is closer to a cash flow concept of income.

Managers reported that accounting statements prepared using TOC principles were much easier to understand than conventional accounting reports, and the effects of their actions on the accounting reports made more sense with the variable costing statements. The managers appeared to be aware of the superiority of variable costing information in making decisions using relevant cost concepts. Furthermore, some companies were taking advantage of the simplicity of TOC accounting to compile profit reports more frequently and on a more timely basis. These reports were being used to monitor the performance of the entire system.

TOC companies typically use physical measures rather than financial measures to monitor and control daily operations. At almost all of the sites we visited, standard cost variance reporting had been abandoned. What then is monitored? In a TOC shop, there are usually at least two buffer inventories—one just in front of the constraint to ensure that it does not starve and a shipping buffer to ensure that jobs are shipped on time. The size and contents of these buffers are monitored closely because they can provide early warning signals of problems. For example, the size and content of the buffer in front of the constraint provides valuable information concerning the overall performance of the work stations in front of the constraint. In addition, the efficiency, downtime, and use of the constraint typically are monitored because any time wasted or lost on a constraint results in a loss of throughput and profits.

In contrast, such measures are *not* used to evaluate performance at nonconstraint work centers. Indeed, there *should* be less than 100% utilization of resources that are not constraints. And there *should* be considerable downtime on nonconstraints due to setups and split batches. Managers in TOC companies believe that the usual standard cost variance reporting control system leads people to take actions that are very nearly the *opposite* of the actions that should be taken.

Management accounting data can be used to help manage a production constraint although we did not see it happen very often at the sites we visited. The contribution margin per unit of the constrained resource is a key financial measure that is critical in two important decisions—prioritizing use of the constraint and deciding whether or not to elevate the constraint. Those products with the smallest contribution margin per unit of the constraint should receive the lowest priority; they are the least valuable use of the constraint. In addition, the contribution margin per unit of the constraint for the marginal job (i.e., the opportunity cost of using the constrained resource) provides a measure of the value of elevating the constraint. (If the next job has a contribution margin per hour of $510, then it would be profitable for the company to spend up to $510 per hour to acquire more of the constrained resource.) If the benefit of elevating the constraint exceeds the cost, then more of the constrained resource should be acquired.

In addition, the opportunity cost of using the constrained resource provides valuable data for pricing products. When there is a production constraint, the real cost of accepting an order is its out-of-pocket variable cost plus the opportunity cost involved in using the constrained resource. Conventional absorption product costs are simply irrelevant in this situation. The actual price charged should depend, of course, on market conditions, the customer, and competition, but, in the absence of countervailing reasons, the price should at least cover out-of-pocket variable costs plus opportunity cost.

To summarize thus far, TOC is a radically different way to control operations and does not work with conventional accounting systems that emphasize cost absorption and standard cost variance analysis. TOC requires major modifications in financial and management accounting systems. TOC also has implications for basic management strategy. In the TOC world, there are only three ways to increase profits:

- Increase throughput (sales);
- Decrease operating expenses (fixed costs); or
- Decrease investment—particularly in inventories.

TOC practitioners tend to put much more emphasis on increasing throughput and decreasing investment than on cutting costs. The basic reason is that really effective cost cutting programs almost inevitably will result in laying off employees, which creates a "Catch-22" situation. Effective cost cutting programs such as TQM require the active and enthusiastic participation of employees. However, employees are unlikely to sustain interest in improvement programs if they observe that improvement leads to layoffs.

TOC managers prefer to find new business when improvement in processes exposes excess capacity or surplus resources. This preference for more business over cutting costs in TOC is not just wishful thinking. TOC supports greater product diversity and greater volume in two ways:

■ It improves operations so that the existing resources can handle greater diversity and volume.

■ TOC accounting provides managers with more pricing flexibility because product costs are much lower under TOC accounting than conventional absorption costing.[1]

In principle, there is a preference in TOC for entering new markets to increase throughput rather than for capturing more market share in existing markets. Such action avoids putting too many eggs in one basket and retaliation by competitors. Therefore, product diversity is encouraged in TOC, in marked contrast to activity-based costing (ABC). ABC usually discourages product diversity by shifting overhead costs to low-volume products, which then appear less profitable. In TOC, the default assumption is that overhead functions, like other nonconstraint work centers, can handle additional diversity without new resources. If they cannot, the overhead resources themselves become the constraint and can be dealt with using the usual TOC approaches. That is, improvement efforts can be focused on that part of overhead that is the constraint. And more resources can be acquired if justified by cost/benefit criteria, and so on. At the sites we visited very few managers seemed concerned about problems of creeping overhead. For the most part, they seemed to be able to diversify and increase volume with relatively modest increases in overhead.

There is potential danger in slavishly focusing all improvement efforts on the constraint. It may be possible to reengineer nonconstraint processes to free up considerable resources, which then can be redeployed profitably. Such opportunities may be overlooked if managers neglect the nonconstraints. In practice, this situation did not seem to exist. While managers clearly were most interested in improving processes at the constraint itself, most of them also pointed with pride to improvements that had been made in nonconstraint processes. Our general impression is that, in terms of process improvements, TOC managers tend to pluck the low-lying fruit on the nonconstraints and to go after the more difficult-to-reach fruit on the constraint itself. This approach seems to be a perfectly sensible way of allocating attention and effort.

In sum, TOC accounting differs dramatically from the accounting found in most manufacturing companies. Most TOC companies use an extreme form of variable costing in which the only costs assigned to products are direct materials. Financial reports are consequently much simpler and easier to understand and can be compiled more quickly and frequently than conventional financial reports. Standard cost variance reporting is abandoned in TOC because it is considered inimical to well-functioning operations. Instead, operational controls focus on physical measures such as the state of the buffer in front of the constraint, which provides an indication of the overall performance of the nonconstrained work centers in front of the constraint.

In a TOC system much more emphasis should be placed on the contribution margin per unit of the constrained resource. This key statistic provides valuable information for prioritizing the use of the constraint, for pricing, and for decisions about acquiring additional resources. TOC provides an orderly, focused process for continual improvement, and its strategic implications differ radically from the implications of activity-based costing.

As the reader is no doubt aware, few of the management accounting techniques found in TOC are completely new. Variable costing has been advocated for decades as an internal reporting alternative to absorption costing. Relevant cost analysis is no stranger to management accountants. Introductory management accounting textbooks routinely include material on the use of the contribution margin per unit of the scarce resource to ration a scarce resource. In recent years some management accountants have been pointing out the dangers of overreliance on standard cost variance reporting systems.

Nevertheless, TOC does make three important contributions. First, viewed from its perspective, oft-neglected management accounting tools such as variable costing and relevant costing appear even more important than generally supposed. For example, in light of what we now know about the problems created by excess inventories, the arguments in favor of variable costing seem even stronger. The problem of managing constrained resources—usually relegated to a few pages in our textbooks—appears to be far more widespread and central to success than previously thought.

Second, TOC provides a coherent and focused management theory within which management accountants can ply their trade. With TOC, management's information requirements are clear, and there is less need for management accountants to second-guess what managers want or to impose on managers systems that they don't want.

Third, for those of us who teach management accounting, it is encouraging to find companies that routinely use many of the techniques we advocate, such as variable costing and relevant costing, which so often seem to be at odds with ordinary practice.

Note

1. Eli Goldratt would like to purge the term "product cost" from our vocabulary—probably because it is more or less synonymous in many managers' minds with conventional absorption costing. We see his point but have difficulty discussing some issues without referring to a concept such as product cost.

The Theory of Constraints and Its Implications for Management Accounting

1 Introduction _____

"Ultimately, success depends upon being able to take the successful ideas and strategies from the great companies and share them with the rest of the economy in real time, with little or no loss in translation." [Curt Reimann, director of the Malcolm Baldrige National Quality Award][1]

The purpose of this study is to summarize the Theory of Constraints (TOC)—particularly those aspects that have not yet appeared in public sources—and to report our observations from visiting a number of sites at which TOC concepts have been put into practice.

The Theory of Constraints was introduced in 1984 in *The Goal,* written by Eliyahu M. Goldratt and Jeff Cox.[2] This unusual book expounded a management theory in the guise of a novel about a plant manager named Alex Rogo. Alex's plant was in deep trouble and in imminent danger of being closed by top management. The plant was rescued by overthrowing time-honored and cherished management practices that were creating devastating problems. Alex was helped along the way by probing questions posed by Jonah, an Israeli academic who appeared at critical points in the novel.

In *The Goal,* the company's traditional cost accounting and variance reporting system was responsible for many of the problems the factory was experiencing. Instead of focusing efforts on activities that would increase profits, the company's traditional management accounting system focused attention mainly on counterproductive

1

efforts to reduce unit product costs. If real improvements had been made in operations, the management accounting system almost invariably would have sent inappropriate signals in the form of unfavorable cost variances. Therefore, as a precondition to improving, Alex had to throw out the old cost accounting and variance reporting systems. He then completely redesigned the accounting and performance reporting system from the ground up.

The Goal poses a challenge for management accountants. Are our traditional systems, including absorption costing and standard cost variance reports, the source of the problem? One controller has candidly admitted that "by hounding our manufacturing department about efficiencies and standard cost variances, I often moved the company away from rather than toward our goal. Because I had ignored our system constraints and relied on traditional standard cost calculations, past decisions made to outsource production and pricing our product were often wrong."[3] If existing management accounting practices are creating problems, what should we do to improve them? How would an accounting system such as the one suggested in *The Goal* operate? Is it practical, or does it suffer from inherent weaknesses?

While the business press has reported sporadically about companies that have implemented ideas from *The Goal*, there has been no systematic study of such firms.[4] Moreover, very little has been reported about companies that have been involved in the newest aspects of TOC, which go far beyond the concepts that can be gleaned from reading *The Goal* or any other publicly available source. This study attempts to remedy both of those deficiencies.

The cigar-smoking Israeli academic in *The Goal* called Jonah bears a striking resemblance to Eliyahu M. Goldratt, the book's principal author and the central figure in the development of TOC. Goldratt has a doctorate in physics and became involved in business almost accidentally. A friend was having difficulty scheduling work at a plant that built chicken coops. Goldratt was intrigued by the problem and conceived an innovative scheduling system that permitted a dramatic increase in completed chicken coops with no increase in operating expenses. Goldratt discovered that there was no satisfactory job shop scheduling software available on the market, so he incorporated his ideas in a software product called OPT that was launched in 1978.

OPT was not part of our investigation, but our impression is that the program was only a modest success at best, and there were a few very unhappy clients.[5] We don't know what caused this dissatisfaction, but we would guess that OPT failed when it was installed in plants where operations were inherently unstable and unpredictable due to the way in which they were being managed or in plants where top management did not fully support the implicit goals of OPT— which often run counter to goals such as cost minimization. This episode tarnished Goldratt's reputation, but he learned that operations must be improved and stabilized before a successful scheduling system can be installed. Grafting a scheduling system onto a chaotic operating system does not solve the problem and may even make it worse. Managers develop coping mechanisms to deal with the chaos on the factory floor. Many of these mechanisms (such as expediting) require frequent disruptions of the schedule. Imposing a schedule in such situations and demanding some discipline in following it may well make matters worse. (Witness the many failures of MRP.) In order to install any scheduling system successfully, it may be necessary to solve much more basic problems first. This insight led to the development of the more general management tools introduced in *The Goal.*

The foregoing story is typical of the way in which TOC has evolved—it has become steadily more general. In each phase of its evolution, at some point further progress in companies is blocked by some higher-order problem. Before a scheduling system can be installed, operations must be stabilized. Before operations can be stabilized, counterproductive policies must be altered. Before counterproductive policies can be altered, they must be identified. And so on. Therefore, it became necessary to develop tools to deal with very general higher-order problems—particularly the sorts of problems that result from inappropriate policies. The latest set of tools, called the "Thinking Process," is very general. The claim is made that it can be applied successfully to virtually any problem from the shop floor to the executive suite—and even to personal problems.

The Avraham Y. Goldratt Institute

The Avraham Y. Goldratt Institute (AGI) and its associates run various educational and training programs ranging from a few hours to several weeks in length. (The foundation is named after Avraham Y. Goldratt, Eli Goldratt's father, one of the founding members of the Israeli parliament.) The AGI views its mission as purely educational—teaching people how to invent their own solutions. For two reasons it resists getting involved in conventional consulting work in which the consultant supplies solutions.[6] First, the client is likely to have better intuition about his own situation than a consultant. Second, solutions almost always involve changes that will be resisted within the organization. Goldratt believes the best way to overcome natural resistance to change is for the people who must make the change to discover their own solution.

The flagship course put on by the AGI is the two-week "Jonah course," which is intended to train people to function like the character Jonah in *The Goal*. Graduates of this course are called Jonahs. This terminology is one of the aspects of the Theory of Constraints that turn off some people. There appears to be something cult-like about a course whose purpose is to create clones of a fictional character patterned after the leader of the movement. Moreover, a secret language is used by the initiated—terms such as the "Thinking Process," "Current Reality Tree," "UDEs," "Drum-Buffer-Rope," and "Evaporating Cloud." This language is more than some people can tolerate. Nevertheless, we advise patience and an open mind. Despite appearances, it really isn't a cult. And while the jargon does get a bit thick at times, most of it is really necessary. Such jargon, by compressing a complex set of ideas into a single term, makes communication more efficient.

With regard to the jargon, we have generally followed the convention of capitalizing words and phrases that have a special meaning in the Theory of Constraints. It may seem pretentious at times, but we feel it helps to keep things straight.

Our study

In order to identify suitable sites for interviewing, we attended two conferences sponsored by the Avraham Y. Goldratt Institute. The first was held in the Netherlands in October 1992, and the second was held in Detroit in February 1993. Both conferences were organized for graduates of the Jonah course. We were introduced on both occasions by Eli Goldratt, who endorsed the study. We then took a few minutes to explain the purposes of the study. We also assured companies that any information they provided to us would be released only with their permission. And we said that there would be no cost to the company apart from taking the time to talk with us. In Europe, where there was a small group, we simply took the names of those who indicated a willingness to cooperate. In Detroit, where hundreds were attending the conference, we used a form to solicit volunteers. From these initial contacts we eventually visited 20 different companies, one of which had three different sites. Five of the companies were located in Belgium and the Netherlands, and the remainder were scattered about the United States.

Some potential biases result from the way in which the sites were chosen. First, only those who found the Jonah course valuable were likely to have attended one of the conferences. Second, only a fraction of the attendees at the conferences volunteered to cooperate in the study. It is likely that those who volunteered considered them-

selves more successful in their use of TOC than those who did not
volunteer. Because we did not have a random sample of companies
involved with TOC, one should be cautious in drawing conclusions
about its success on the basis of our sample.

All of the sites we visited were involved in manufacturing, and
almost all were traditional job shop operations. Some of the aspects
of TOC (for example, Drum-Buffer-Rope scheduling) are more applicable to job shop environments than to other environments in
manufacturing or service industries. However, most of TOC has much
broader application. We suspect that the preponderance of job shop
sites in our sample simply reflects the fact that most people are introduced to TOC by reading *The Goal*, which has a job shop setting.

Most of the sites were single-location, privately held companies
with fewer than a couple of hundred employees. A few were manufacturing subsidiaries of Fortune 500 companies. We typically interviewed
the top general manager and production managers at each site. At
the privately held companies, the top manager was usually an owner
of the company.

The rest of the book

For the reader who wants more than the compact executive summary of our main findings provided at the beginning of the book,
Chapter 2 gives a detailed overview of the theory and practice of
TOC. And for the reader who wants even more details about the
specifics of what we found at the most interesting companies we
visited, Chapter 3 will provide the particulars. Chapter 4 gives further observations and conclusions, based on our personal opinions.
Finally, because no description of the Thinking Process is publicly
available, we have written an introduction to this intriguing development. It is included as an appendix in this monograph.

Notes

1. Curt W. Reimann, "Establishing Quality Initiatives," *Sustaining Total Quality*, The Conference Board, 1993, p. 16.

2. Eliyahu M. Goldratt and Jeff Cox, *The Goal: A Process of Ongoing Improvement*, North River Press, Croton-on-Hudson, N.Y., 1984. The various editions of *The Goal* have sold more than 1,750,000 copies in 16 different languages.

3. David S. Koziol, "How the Constraint Theory Improved a Job Shop Operation," *Management Accounting*, May 1988, p. 49.

4. See, for example, the following articles: Susan Jayson, "Goldratt & Fox: Revolutionizing the Factory Floor," *Management Accounting*, May 1987, pp. 18-22.

Martha E. Mangelsdorf, "What Chief Executives Read," *Inc. Magazine*, September 1990, pp. 64-80.

Kim D. Shaver, "This quiet revolution shatters the cost world: TOC's cashflow approach slices inventory, boosts bottom line," *Furniture Today*, August 26, 1991, p. 20.

Harper A. Roehm, Donald J. Klein, and Joseph F. Castellano, "Springing to World-Class Manufacturing," *Management Accounting*, March 1991, pp. 40-44.

John Darlington, John Innes, Falconer Mitchell, and John Woodward, "Throughput Accounting: the Garret Automotive Experience," *Management Accounting* (U.K.), April 1992, pp. 32-38.

James T. Mackey, editor, *Cases from Management Accounting Practice*, Volume 8, Institute of Management Accountants, Montvale, New Jersey, 1992.

5. The results of a survey of 22 firms that had been involved in OPT are reported in Timothy D. Fry, James F. Cox, and John H. Blackstone Jr., "An Analysis and Discussion of the Optimized Production Technology Software and Its Use," *Production and Operations Management*, Spring 1992, pp. 229-242. The average rating for the "quality of schedule" was 2.9 on a four-point scale, where 1 indicated poor performance; 2, fair performance; 3, good performance; and 4, excellent performance.

6. At the time of this writing, a reorganization was underway at the Avraham Goldratt Institute. Some of the associates of the AGI were forming a new firm that would take a more conventional consulting approach using the TOC framework. The AGI itself would continue to be primarily an educational institute.

2 The Theory of Constraints in Theory and in Practice ___

Introduction

In this chapter we discuss the theory and practice of "traditional TOC"—elements of TOC that should be somewhat familiar to those who have read *The Goal*. We also consider the Thinking Process, which goes far beyond the ideas contained in *The Goal*. We begin this chapter with a discussion of the role of inventories in operations because it directly affects the nature of TOC accounting. We then discuss how accounting measures are used in TOC to make decisions and to control operations. We pay particular attention to the distinctive elements of TOC that differentiate it from other improvement programs—Drum-Buffer-Rope scheduling and constraint management. We then discuss in very broad terms the Thinking Process; more details are available in the Appendix. In addition to explaining the basics of TOC theory, we will be making observations based on our site visits about how TOC works in practice.

The effects of excess inventories on operations

The underlying premise in much of TOC is that the goal of most companies is to make more money now and in the future. Money is generated by selling goods and services to customers. Money is not generated by building inventories, although some inventories are necessary to ensure timely deliveries to customers. However, excessive inventories—particularly work-in-process inventories—are an operating liability. TOC and the just-in-time (JIT) movement are in agreement that work-in-process inventories can create big operating problems that dwarf the more obvious holding costs associated with inventories. Inventories both create and hide operational inefficiencies and problems. TOC and JIT strive to eliminate excess work-in-process inventories and to improve processes so that less inventory needs to be held as insurance against unforeseen problems.

Companies that have higher work-in-process inventories than their competitors are at a serious disadvantage for a variety of reasons. Cycle times and lead times decrease almost automatically with reductions in excess work-in-process inventories. If a plant has six weeks of work-in-process inventory sitting idle at any time, then on average it will take at least six weeks for a job to be completed from beginning to end in addition to its actual processing time. Therefore, decreasing the size of work-in-process inventory almost automatically decreases cycle times and lead times.

In addition, large work-in-process inventories make it difficult to track down the causes of defects and correct them before further damage can be done. Quite often defects are caught only at the final inspection point, after the last operation. If work-in-process is high and cycle times are long, a defect may be undetected for weeks or even months. Who will be able to recall what the operating conditions were at the time? What will have happened to other parts that were processed at the same time and were also vulnerable to the same operating problems? And if the defective unit must be scrapped, there will be great pressure to expedite a new unit through the entire system to complete the order. If this situation happens frequently, management may react by routinely producing more units than have been ordered "just in case" defects show up late in the process, or management may invest more resources in detecting defects earlier in the process.

A company with higher work-in-process inventories than its competitors probably also will have to expedite orders more frequently. Because work-in-process inventories add to lead time, a company with higher work-in-process inventories than a competitor will have longer lead times than the competitor. Suppose, for example, that the higher work-in-process inventory company has a lead time of four months whereas the lower work-in-process company has a lead time of three months. To remain competitive in the market, the company with the higher work-in-process inventories will sometimes have to accept orders with a lead time of less than four months. Such orders will require expediting and may involve additional spending for items such as overtime to meet the delivery date.

The same phenomenon is responsible for planning problems and poor due date performance at high work-in-process inventory companies. If competitors with lower work-in-process inventories have a three-month lead time, customers may view this length of time as the industry standard and may feel free to change their orders up to three months before the due date. These changes do not cause problems at the companies with low work-in-process inventories and lead times of three months, but notice what happens at the high work-in-process inventory company whose lead time is four months. It will be thrown into crisis situations regularly by customers who change their orders a month after production has begun on the order. This effect leads to planning problems and poor due date performance. This particular problem is most severe in an environment in which each job is unique. If a single homogeneous product is being made, changes in orders can be accommodated out of inventories.

Goldratt and Fox sum up this line of reasoning as follows: "It's no wonder that due-date performance is a problem where we have high inventories. When we operate in a lower inventory mode than our competitors, we enjoy an enviable position that gives us an inherently more accurate forecast. Now when we start production, we have firm orders or a valid forecast which is much less likely to change. Our due-date performance will be much improved."[1] Therefore, reduction of excess work-in-process inventories may be crucial in markets where due date performance is very important.

In summary, excess inventories can increase cycle time, decrease due date performance, increase defect rates, increase operating expenses, reduce the ability to plan, and ultimately reduce sales and profits. These effects of high inventories will be more pronounced in some companies than in others. For example, as we observed above, poor due date performance is more likely to be a problem when each job is unique. At any rate, because excess inventories can create so many problems, Goldratt is against accounting practices that provide artificial incentives to build inventories.

Throughput Accounting

It is well known that any system such as full absorption costing that capitalizes fixed costs in inventories creates incentives to build inventories and to manipulate inventory levels to smooth income.[2] This argument was made decades ago by opponents of absorption costing. However, even the opponents of absorption costing probably did not realize the extent of the problems created by excessive inventories—particularly work-in-process inventories. Inventory holding costs are just the tip of the iceberg. Largely because absorption costing rewards managers for building inventories, Goldratt rejects it in favor of a variation of variable (i.e., direct) costing that he calls Throughput Accounting.

Goldratt's accounting system has three building blocks: throughput, operating expenses, and assets.[3] Throughput is defined as the rate at which the system generates money (i.e., incremental cash flows) through sales. Assets are defined as all the money the system invests in purchasing things the system intends to sell. Operating expenses are defined as all the money the system spends in turning inventory into throughput. These published definitions are too vague to be operational, so we have relied on conversations with Goldratt and our site visits to refine what these terms mean.

The official current definition of throughput is revenue less "totally variable costs." However, in most of the TOC literature, throughput has been defined as revenue less direct materials. In practice, we observed both versions in use. Some companies deduct only direct materials from revenue to arrive at throughput, whereas others deduct other variable costs such as subcontracting work, variable selling costs, and variable shipping costs. The simplified version may be used because there are no significant variable costs other than direct materials. We suspect, however, that some managers have adopted the simpler definition just because it is the definition used in most of the TOC literature. We did not pursue this question in our field investigations.

Assets in Throughput Accounting are identical to assets in conventional financial accounting except for inventories. Inventories in Throughput Accounting, as in variable costing, consist solely of totally variable costs that already have been incurred on behalf of items in inventory.

Operating expenses consist of all of the expenses that are not deducted in arriving at throughput. The sum of operating expenses and deductions from revenue in determining throughput is identical to the sum of the expenses recognized on the income statement under conventional full absorption costing—except for changes in the additional costs capitalized in inventories under conventional financial accounting.

At the conceptual level, throughput is indistinguishable from the contribution margin. Throughput is revenue less "totally variable costs," and the general definition of the contribution margin is revenue less variable costs. Also at the conceptual level there is no difference between Throughput Accounting and variable costing. In practice, however, there is one significant difference—the treatment of direct labor. In Throughput Accounting, direct labor is not deducted when computing throughput and is not capitalized in inventories. Instead, it is included as part of operating expense. The conventional treatment in variable costing is to consider direct labor a variable cost. However, it is just a convention, and if labor is considered to be fixed under variable costing, then variable costing would be identical to Throughput Accounting apart from the way a few accounts are labelled.

The essential differences between variable costing and Throughput Accounting are summarized in Exhibit 2-1. It is easy to understand why direct labor traditionally has been treated as a variable cost in illustrations of variable costing. When variable costing originally was conceived and first introduced in textbooks, direct labor was a variable cost in most organizations. Piece rates were com-

Exhibit 2-1
Comparison of Variable Costing with Throughput Accounting

Conventional variable costing	Variable costing with direct labor classified as fixed	Throughput Accounting	Simplified Throughput Accounting
Revenue	Revenue	Revenue	Revenue
-Direct materials	-Direct materials	-Totally variable costs	-Direct materials
-Direct labor			
-Variable overhead*	-Variable overhead*		
=Contrib. margin	=Contrib. margin	=Throughput	=Throughput
-Fixed expenses	-Fixed expenses	-Oper. expenses	-Oper. expenses
=Profit	=Profit	=Profit	=Profit

*Variable overhead, both production and nonproduction

mon, and management felt much freer to adjust the direct labor workforce. Now management is often reluctant to lay off direct labor workers (particularly those with special skills) except under dire circumstances. Hence it can be argued that today in many organizations direct labor is essentially a fixed cost—particularly in the short run. In fact, some companies now consider direct labor a part of fixed overhead. Consistent with this viewpoint, unless labor is on a piece rate, Goldratt classifies direct labor as operating expense (and hence fixed).

Despite Goldratt's general insistence that direct labor should not be deducted when computing throughput, we did find several TOC sites where this advice is ignored. One site had gone through a radical downsizing prior to involvement in TOC and was slowly adjusting its remaining workforce. Despite increased production volume, it was continuing to shrink employment through natural attrition. It was able to increase volume with a smaller total workforce by applying TOC and TQM techniques and by converting overhead staff into direct labor. The manager argued that in his company direct labor is a variable cost and should be a deduction in the calculation of throughput. At another site, direct labor is considered part of totally variable costs when winning a contract leads to hiring more direct labor.

Apart from the issue of which costs should be capitalized in inventories, there is only one other area where Throughput Accounting departs from conventional financial accounting practice. Goldratt is a conservative when it comes to revenue recognition issues:

> In many consumer-goods industries, the products are not sold directly to the consumer by the manufacturer, but rather through distribution chains. In most cases, those distribution channels reserve the right to return merchandise without even an explanation. It seems very inappropriate that a sale is recorded when products are shipped to the distribution companies, even though the transaction is certainly reversible. . . . The sale should be

recorded when an irrevocable transaction has occurred with the consumer. . . . Excess products in the distribution pipes just increase the distance between the producer and its ultimate client. This is almost a recipe for a future loss in throughput.[4]

In the context of the history of management accounting thought, Goldratt has simply updated variable costing and is conservative with respect to revenue recognition. He advocates variable costing for the same reasons it always has been advocated—it is closer to cash flows, can be used more easily than absorption costing to estimate relevant costs and benefits, and, most important, does not contain incentives to build inventories just to improve absorption costing profits. The argument is even more valid now than in the 1950s when arguments were raging concerning absorption and variable costing. We now know that excess work-in-process inventories are a much bigger problem than anyone had thought. Not only are there inventory holding costs and obsolescence problems, but work-in-process inventories create big problems on the factory floor. Any system such as absorption costing that rewards managers for building inventories to manipulate profits can be far more dysfunctional than even the critics of the 1950s imagined.

Most of the sites we visited had adopted some form of Throughput Accounting, and most were preparing reports at least monthly. In a few cases, throughput was being reported daily. This ability is a particular strength of TOC. Financial results can be reported and communicated very quickly and cheaply, and the accounting system is simple enough that the financial results can be understood easily on the shop floor.

The system in use at one company was particularly interesting. Each month a graph is drawn with dollars on the vertical axis and the working days of the month on the horizontal axis. A blue line is drawn from zero up to the budgeted throughput for the month. This line serves as the standard. Cumulative actual throughput for the month is plotted in red on the same graph. The difference between the red and blue lines quickly conveys variance from budget to date.

Managers were satisfied with the clarity, simplicity, and understandability of the Throughput Accounting reports and in no case had any nostalgia for the reporting systems that had been discarded. Managers at many sites reported that an immediate effect of converting to Throughput Accounting was greater freedom in pricing decisions. Reported margins are much larger under Throughput Accounting than under absorption accounting, so managers felt less reluctant to lower prices to pursue attractive opportunities. Of course, there are risks along with this freedom. The freedom to lower prices under variable costing (and Throughput Accounting) often is cited by critics as a potential pitfall, although Goldratt warns against cutting prices to gain market share. To increase throughput without exposing the company to retaliation by competitors and overexposure to the risks of downturns in a single market, Goldratt advocates entering new markets and diversifying product offerings.

Managers at one of the companies we visited said that, acting contrary to this advice, they had made the mistake of substantially cutting prices on standard products with well-established market prices. They got a lot more business for about a month, and then competitors responded and the market has yet to recover. The company now accepts the market price on such standard products and uses its pricing discretion to win bids it really wants on custom-made products that have no established market price.

For reasons we cannot follow, managers at another site claim that they used Throughput Accounting to justify a strategy of moving downscale in the market. They were shifting their production from premium products to commodity products, and they were cutting their prices. At the time of our visit, this strategy was running into problems because competitors were lowering their prices in response.

With these two exceptions, managers were quite pleased with the pricing flexibility provided by Throughput Accounting, and some were using this flexibility to enter lucrative new markets. Some managers also were coordinating their pricing policies to even out the load on the constraint.

For example, one company was giving price breaks for longer lead times, so the company could fit in long-lead jobs on a piecemeal basis as opportunities arose. Other managers were giving price breaks for orders during slack periods. Of course, such practices are not uncommon in traditional cost-oriented companies, but the rationale is different. In a cost-oriented company, price breaks are given to get enough business to "keep everyone busy." In a TOC company, price breaks are given to increase profits. The price breaks are possible because when the constraint would otherwise be idle, there is no opportunity cost.

A few companies had experienced difficulties in implementing Throughput Accounting because of the requirement that revenue (throughput) be recorded only when a product is sold. At one company the requirement created problems in calculating profits at the plant level because some products are made by more than one plant, but once a unit enters the central warehouse it loses its identity. Thus, when a unit is sold, there is no way of knowing which plant made it. In addition, there were concerns about changes in selling prices that occur between the time a product is made and the time it is sold. Because of these technical difficulties, the attempt to use Throughput Accounting was abandoned, and the company retained its old system of crediting the plants at full standard cost for whatever they ship.

A few sites were using Throughput Accounting in external financial reports, but it is important to note that these companies are privately held. Most of the companies we visited had not even attempted to switch to Throughput Accounting for external reports. In several cases, managers who had attempted to switch were blocked by auditors or by an external party such as a banker.

Given the similarity between Throughput Accounting and variable costing and the contribution margin approach, it should not be surprising that relevant cost analysis is used in TOC—although it is not called by that name.

TOC and relevant cost analysis

As in many other areas, TOC is highly consistent with traditional management accounting approaches that are routinely taught even in introductory management accounting courses. For example, Goldratt's discussion of the product drop decision is virtually indistinguishable (except for the different terms used) from the discussion that can be found in just about any management accounting textbook. Both Goldratt and the textbooks focus on identifying the relevant costs and benefits associated with a decision. He cautions against the use of fully allocated product costs in such decisions, as do management accounting textbooks, and advises that every major decision should be evaluated based on its impact on both throughput and operating expenses (and assets if applicable).

Goldratt discusses dropping a product in the following passage:

> By trimming the above product, we would know how much the Throughput is reduced. . . . What we have to consider now is the impact of trimming that product on the Operating expenses. How many people will we be able to lay off (not just in production but also in sales, engineering, and administration)? We want names. It's impossible to lay off three minutes of a worker. If we are just going to transfer them to another department, then we would like to know how much the Throughput can be expected to increase there. Just moving people from one department to another does not reduce the Operating Expense. If the resulting reduction in Operating Expense is larger than the reduction in Throughput, trimming the product will definitely increase the Net Profit of the company. If it's smaller, it will certainly reduce the Net Profit . . . .[5]

Managers at a number of sites we visited stated that they now are evaluating alternatives based primarily on the impacts on throughput, operating expenses, and assets. Previously, such decisions had been made informally or on the basis of direct labor and overhead reduction calculations or reductions in absorption unit costs. This emphasis on identifying relevant costs and benefits was most highly formalized at Western Textile Products (described in Chapter 3) where a standardized evaluation form had been developed.

TOC control measures

In TOC, profits are measured by throughput less operating expenses and profitability by profits divided by assets. Therefore, controls center on throughput, operating expenses, and assets. Managers are expected to follow the global plan, which is to ship specific orders by specific dates using no more than a specific level of operating expenses and capacities and a specific level of inventories. Any unauthorized tinkering with the plan is likely to have unforeseen consequences elsewhere, so emphasis is placed on following the plan. Therefore, the controls take the global plan as given and attempt to assess how well the plan was executed. Throughput-dollar-days measures failures to ship specific orders by specific dates. Local-operating-expense measures variances between actual and planned spending. Inventory-dollar-days measures excess inventories. These measures are intended to control operations and do not necessarily articulate with financial accounting measures.

The local-operating-expense measure recognizes responsibility accounting issues well known in the management accounting literature. Local area managers should not be held responsible for expenses that occur outside of their area of control—particularly allocated central administration expenses. Unfortunately, apart from this general admonition against allocations of uncontrollable costs, there are no specific guidelines in the TOC literature about how this local-operating-expense control actually would work. Should actual expenses be compared to the previous period's expenses? To budgeted expenses? To some sort of flexible budget? There are no answers to these questions in the TOC literature.

In practice, actual operating expenses were compared to the previous period's operating expenses at some sites and to fixed budgets at others. Very few sites were big enough to have more than a single operating expense control report for the entire site. With one exception, in the few instances in which a multisite company had adopted TOC, there was no allocation of central administrative overhead to lower levels in the organization. Responsibility accounting principles generally were being followed. The emphasis was on controlling increases in operating expenses rather than attempting to reduce operating expenses. Any significant reduction in operating expenses almost certainly would involve layoffs, avoided at almost all cost in TOC. More subtly, reductions in operating expenses could cut into the protective capacity on the nonconstraints and have unanticipated consequences such as deteriorating due date performance.

Throughput-dollar-days is an unusual measure of due-date performance. It is computed by assigning to every late order a value equal to its throughput multiplied by the number of days the order is late. Ideally, throughput-dollar-days should be zero because there should be no late orders. The larger the throughput value of the order, the larger the deviation from zero. And the tardier the order, the larger the deviation from zero. Who "owns" the deviation? Goldratt suggests that whichever department currently is processing the order be held responsible for the throughput-dollar-days of the order. While this method may seem unfair—the current department may be late simply because of what happened in prior departments—it nevertheless creates incentives to get the order out the door. As soon as the current department finishes its processing of the order, the throughput-dollar-days becomes the responsibility of the next department. Goldratt likens a late order tagged with the throughput-dollar-days measure to a hot potato that departments are eager to pass on down the line. The larger the size of the order and the later it is, the hotter the potato. While this idea may be appealing in theory, we did not find it in use at any of the sites we visited. When through-put-dollar-days was discussed at all in our visits, it was dismissed as an impractical idea.

Inventory-dollar-days is a measure of excess inventories. Suppose, for example, that 10 days of finished goods inventories are considered sufficient to ensure satisfactory due date performance. Any inventories of finished goods expected to be around after 10 days are considered excess inventories. If there are 120 units of product X in finished goods inventories and the daily sales amount to 10 units, then the excess inventory is 20 units. The seriousness of the excess inventories depends on how much has been invested in the inventories and how long that investment will last. In this example, the excess inventories will be eliminated in two days. That is, two days of sales at the rate of 10 units per day should reduce the inventory to the desired 10-day buffer. Ten units of the excess inventory will be held for one day and 10 units will be held for two days, so the total "excess-inventory-days" would be 30 (10x1 + 10x2). The inventory-dollar-days is computed by multiplying the excess-inventory-days by the value of a unit of inventory. If the inventory is valued at $20 per unit, the inventory-dollar-days for this product would be $600. Ideally, inventory-dollar-days should be zero.

The inventory-dollar-days measure was being used at only one site we visited, Samsonite Europe, which used the measure on its "Not To Do List." Managers at Samsonite Europe commented to us that the inventory-dollar-days measure is often too large to be credible because it is the product of the value of inventory and the number of days it will be outstanding. They suggested that this gross measure, which is denominated in unfamiliar terms, should be modified to measure the costs of holding excess inventory. This modification would involve multiplying the value of excess inventory on each day by a rate designed to reflect holding costs and perhaps operating problems associated with excess inventories. It would effectively reduce the magnitude of the measure.

Instead of the recommended TOC control measures, we found a wide variety of other control measures in use at the sites we visited. For example, some companies controlled "totally variable costs" using some sort of standard unit costs. Some companies were monitoring defect rates. Some were monitoring downtime. Some were monitoring due date performance, and so on. The measures monitored by managers seemed to be dictated by important features of their particular situations.

In most cases, these control measures were consistent with TOC, although not explicitly recommended in the TOC literature. However, some managers were monitoring measures that had potential for misuse. For example, improper use of utilization and efficiency measures for nonconstraints can lead to undesirable behavior such as building excess inventories. However, utilization and efficiency measures for nonconstraints *can* provide useful information. For example, chronically high levels of excess capacity might call for some reduction in fixed assets or for adding new products that can exploit that excess capacity. It would be unwise to use utilization and efficiency measures for nonconstraint resources to evaluate the performance of individuals—it would create undesirable incentives to build excess inventories. We found some evidence of such use in practice. It is always a potential danger if utilization and efficiency measures for nonconstraints are not used with caution.

Goldratt's critique of cost accounting

Like other critics of traditional cost accounting practices (for example, Kaplan and Johnson), Goldratt believes traditional full absorption costing was reasonably accurate in the early days of cost accounting when direct labor was variable and there was little overhead. However, labor now is largely fixed, and overhead has become a large part of total cost. Goldratt parts company with those who advocate activity-based costing as a means of reviving the relevance of cost accounting because he does not believe activity-based costing can provide reliable answers to the question "What impact will this decision have on throughput, operating expenses, and assets?"[6]

To free ourselves from the kind of thinking that leads to fully allocated product costs, Goldratt believes it is necessary to purge the term "product cost" from our vocabulary. He is adamant that there is no such thing in reality as a product cost even though he deducts "totally variable costs" from revenue to arrive at the throughput for a product.

We think he insists on this point because he believes the term product cost is synonymous with fully allocated product costs in the minds of many managers. If managers believe product costs exist, then they will demand that accountants produce fully allocated product costs. Goldratt blames the managers who demand fully allocated product costs—not the accountants who produce them. He seems sympathetic to the plight of accountants who struggle to produce relevant reports that will be accepted by managers with a product cost and cost reduction mindset.

Goldratt observes that the other major improvement programs, TQM and JIT, are no friends of cost accounting either. TQM simply:

> [shoved] aside the financial measurements, stating that 'Quality is Job One.' JIT has done basically the same thing. When I met Dr. Ohno, the inventor of Kanban, the JIT system of Toyota, he told me that cost accounting was the one thing that he had to fight against all his life. 'It was not enough to chase out the cost accountants from the plants, the problem was to chase cost accounting from my people's minds.' [7]

We found a few sites where managers still were trying to rely on their traditional cost accounting systems. Most sites, however, had converted to Throughput Accounting, and there was little evidence that managers still were thinking in terms of fully allocated product costs or were focusing their energies on cost reduction rather than on profit enhancement. Several managers admitted that prior to TOC, they had attempted to control overhead by controlling direct labor but were no longer doing it.

At one of the sites where TOC had run into trouble, conflict had developed between line managers who are TOC oriented and the accounting staff. The line managers had thrown out the old labor efficiency reporting system and were focusing on physical measures such as output.

The cost accounting manager was uncomfortable with this approach and so designed a new reporting system that monitored unit conversion costs at each work cell. He admits that the unit conversion costs are driven primarily by unit volume, which is determined by the production schedule. Nevertheless, he feels that there must be a system for developing unit product costs for pricing decisions and for evaluating brand managers. (Marketing claims that the company is a price-taker and that product costs should not play much role in the pricing decision.)

Over the objections of operating managers, who viewed it as a wasted effort, accounting developed an ABC system with multiple cost pools for the purpose of computing product costs. Under the new ABC system, batch-level costs are rather large. Because brand managers are evaluated based on their brand profitability and apparently are not charged inventory holding costs, brand managers have dictated that products can be made only in large batches or the brand manager will go to an outside vendor.

Operating managers claim that in some cases this directive has resulted in batch sizes equivalent to an entire year's supply of the product. The operating managers assert that these kinds of decisions counter all of the gains they have made in inventory reductions, shorter cycle times, and improved manufacturing flexibility. This suboptimization resulted from inappropriate and mismatched performance measures between marketing and manufacturing.

TOC priorities

The managers at the TOC sites we visited almost unanimously agreed with Goldratt that there is far too much emphasis in most organizations on reducing unit absorption costs and on improving local efficiency at the expense of the health of the entire system. Quite a few managers readily admitted that prior to their involvement in TOC operations were very similar to those in Alex Rogo's plant in *The Goal* before Jonah entered the picture.

If the objective is to make more money now and in the future, in the Goldratt classification scheme there are only three ways to do it: increase throughput, decrease operating expenses, or decrease investment in assets. Goldratt asserts that most organizations focus their improvement efforts on reducing operating expenses. Throughput is viewed as something that is outside the control of the organization—particularly in traditional organizations where manufacturing is decoupled from marketing. Therefore, manufacturing managers like to focus their improvement efforts elsewhere. Assets, except possibly for inventories, are not viewed as evil, so it is difficult to drum up enthusiasm for asset reduction programs. Therefore, Goldratt argues, when embarking on improvement programs most organizations place the emphasis squarely on reducing operating expenses.

There does appear to have been a greatly increased emphasis on operating expense reduction in recent years. It is evidenced by the epidemic of downsizing that has swept through companies. Goldratt alleges that most attempts to reduce operating expenses lack focus. He argues that because operating expenses are incurred everywhere in the organization, almost everything looks important in a campaign to reduce operating expenses. We believe this argument does not give enough credit to managers, many of whom have been struggling to identify value-added and nonvalue-added activities. Nevertheless, most commentators inside and outside of TOC would agree that serious attempts to cut operating expenses may turn out to be counterproductive because they eventually must focus on eliminating employees—with potentially devastating effects on the morale of those who remain.

Goldratt argues that improvement usually should focus on increasing throughput, decreasing inventories, and decreasing operating expenses in that order. The reasons are simple. It is difficult to cut operating expenses without laying off people and damaging the organization. Perhaps people should be redeployed, but redeploying people does not decrease operating expenses; at best it increases throughput. Reducing inventories also ordinarily should take precedence over reducing operating expenses because it will decrease assets and result in an increase in throughput and a decrease in operating expenses. (This is, after all, the major message of the just-in-time movement.) Reducing inventories should be given priority over reducing operating expenses—a common thread in JIT, TQM, and TOC.

Given this shift in priorities, what exactly should be done? Often, throughput can be increased and inventories reduced simply by changing the way in which jobs are scheduled in a job shop, which brings us to the next subject—the Drum-Buffer-Rope system.

The Drum-Buffer-Rope scheduling system

A constraint in a system is anything that limits the system from achieving its objective. Any real system must have at least one constraint, and any profit-making organization must have at least one constraint that prevents it from making more profits. If a system did not have a constraint, its output would be unlimited. It is also true, but less obvious, that physical systems consisting of sequential processing through a chain of resources ordinarily have only one constraint. This situation is easiest to see in a chain that consists of resources with differing capacities. The resource with the least capacity ordinarily will be the constraint. While much less obvious, even chains with balanced resource capacities ordinarily will have only one constraint at any one time. However, in such chains the constraint may float from one resource to another due to changes in product mix and random disruptions.

In the early and mid-1980s, when the Theory of Constraints was being developed, the economy was booming, and most manufacturing companies were unable to keep up with demand. The constraint was in the factory. Therefore TOC initially focused on improving factory operations so that more throughput could be achieved without any significant increase in operating expenses or increases in assets—particularly inventories. The lessons learned from that initial effort are still important, even though the constraint in recent years has shifted to the market in many organizations and has necessitated the development of new TOC tools.

Important features of many production processes were explained in *The Goal* using the analogy of a scout troop on a hike. The trail represents the work to be performed, and the objective is to complete the hike by some set time. The scouts are lined up in single file just like work centers in a factory. As in most production processes, the scouts walk at different average rates. That is, they have differing capacities to process jobs (i.e., walk the trail). The rates at which the scouts walk are subject to variation, and disruptions can occur such as a scout stopping to retrieve something to eat from his pack. The leading scout receives raw material (i.e., untraversed trail). The material is processed sequentially (i.e., walked on) by the subsequent scouts in the line. The last scout in the line releases the finished goods (i.e., the trail that has been traversed by everyone in the troop). In this analogy, work-in-process inventory is distance between the leading scout and the last scout in the line. When the troop sets out on the hike, the scouts will be tightly bunched. However, unless the slowest scout is placed near the front of the line, the troop will begin to spread apart quickly, and within a few miles there will be big gaps in the line. These gaps will continue to spread and the distance between the leading scout and the last scout in the line will continue to grow; the analogy is that the work-in-process inventory will grow. This spreading is due to statistical fluctuations in walking rates and to differences in the natural walking abilities of the scouts. This phenomenon also is found on the shop floor. The troop will not be finished with the hike until the last scout in the line is finished. The problem is to reduce the spreading (work-in-process inventory) without increasing the total time to complete the hike.

One solution is to arrange the scouts in order of their walking rates, with the slowest scout (i.e., machine with the least capacity) in the front of the troop. This order minimizes spreading and the total time required for the troop to complete the hike. Such a solution would be expensive, however, and perhaps infeasible on the shop floor. It would require restructuring the plant so that the first work center is the one with the least capacity (i.e., the slowest). Subsequent operations would have to be modified so that each work center has greater capacity than its predecessor. In addition, this solution may not be stable. Changes in the product mix may result in some operation other than the first being the most heavily loaded. When this occurs, it is called a "floating bottleneck."

Another solution is to tie all of the scouts together with a rope like mountain climbers or have a leader count cadence to keep everyone walking at the same rate. This is essentially what Henry Ford did with his assembly line. By putting the work-in-process on a conveyor, he made sure that all work centers were operating at the same effective rate. The Kanban system used in just-in-time is a clever variation on this method.

The assembly line and Kanban systems establish a predetermined inventory buffer (rope length) between each two work centers. On the assembly line, the buffer is the space on the conveyor belt between the operations. In the Kanban system, the buffer is determined by the number of units specified on the Kanban card and the number of Kanban cards maintained in front of the work station.

The state of the buffer *following* a work center signals when work should begin and when it should stop at that work center. Work should begin only when the buffer has been depleted and should stop as soon as it is refilled. Thus work is pulled through the shop. Both the assembly line and Kanban systems are designed to synchronize the work flow so that inventories can be very low compared to conventional shop floor control systems.

The major drawback to JIT or assembly line operations is that any disruption at any work station will cause the entire line to stop. The protective buffers in front of each work station are very small, so when a disruption hits one work station, all work stations will quickly exhaust their protective buffers and the entire line will grind to a halt. Simple variation in processing times creates problems. Because of statistical fluctuations, the overall rate of throughput in a linked system without protective buffers can be far less than even the average rate of the slowest work center in the system. For this reason, an essential part of any conversion to a JIT or assembly line operation is to squeeze variation out of each individual process—hence the emphasis on statistical process control, routine maintenance, and other factors in JIT systems. The sources of disruptions and fluctuations must be dealt with, or the overall throughput in a JIT system may be even less than before JIT was installed. Returning to the scout troop analogy, the JIT solution to the problem of minimizing spreading while ensuring the entire troop finishes the hike on time is to level the hills, pave the trails, improve the hiking boots, and train (or constrain) all of the scouts to walk at exactly the same pace.

The TOC solution begins with the premise that different resources have different capacities and that statistical fluctuations and disruptions cannot realistically be eliminated. Any viable solution must be able to cope with these facts of life. The solution, called Drum-Buffer-Rope (DBR), is to tie a rope between the leading scout and the slowest scout in the line (i.e., the constraint). The leading scout then never can get more than the length of the rope ahead of the slowest scout, and the scouts behind the slowest scout, because they are faster than the slowest scout, can close up any gaps that might temporarily develop. This solution constrains the scouts in front of the slowest scout to walk no faster, on average, than the slowest scout. More important, the length of the rope between the lead scout and the slowest scout is the size of the work-in-process in front of the slowest scout. The rope prevents the work-in-process from growing. Because all of the scouts in front of the slowest scout are faster, they will tend to congregate right behind the lead scout. This tendency will open up a space just in front of the slowest scout that is called the protective buffer. The DBR solution is illustrated in Exhibit 2-2.

This shop floor control method is called Drum-Buffer-Rope because the slowest scout sets the pace (i.e., is the drum). The lead scout is tied to the slowest scout by a rope that enforces the pace, and the overall pace of the troop is protected by the buffer. The DBR solution works best when the slowest scout is significantly slower than all of the other scouts. For reasons that will be explained later, it is very difficult to prevent spreading and to maintain the overall pace of the troop if all the scouts walk at the same average pace (i.e., the plant is perfectly balanced) and those paces are subject to statistical fluctuations.

Exhibit 2-2
An Illustration of Drum-Buffer-Rope

Compare this DBR solution to the assembly line and JIT solutions, which implicitly rope all of the scouts together. On an assembly line or in JIT, if one of the scouts behind the slowest scout gets a stone in his shoe and stops to remove it, the whole line stops. Under the DBR system, this disruption will not threaten the progress of the troop because the scouts in front of the stopped scout can keep walking. Providing that the scouts who are delayed by the disruption have enough reserve speed, they can catch up with the slowest scout. Likewise, if a scout in front of the slowest scout stops, some time will elapse before the slowest scout catches up (i.e., crosses the protective buffer) and the troop must stop.

Translating the scout troop analogy to the shop floor is not difficult. The problem is to provide excellent due date performance while at the same time minimizing inventories. If demand exceeds capacity (i.e., the constraint is in the plant), then there must be at least one "bottleneck" somewhere in the production process. A bottleneck is a resource with insufficient capacity to satisfy demand. There can be more than one bottleneck in a system, but only one is a real constraint. The bottleneck that limits the throughput of the entire system is called a "capacity-constrained resource" or "bottleneck constraint." The essential elements of the DBR solution when the constraint is in the plant are diagrammed in Exhibit 2-3. In the simplest settings, only two events are actually scheduled—the time at which the job will be released to the shop floor and the time at which the job will be loaded onto the bottleneck constraint.

Job scheduling in a DBR system is only of secondary interest to management accountants, so we will not go into the details and all of the complications that can arise. However, the basic ideas are simple and provide some interesting insights. DBR, like JIT, is a demand-pull system. Unlike JIT, DBR does not require extensive fine-tuning throughout the production line because the buffer inventories in DBR are astutely placed to ensure against problems created by statistical fluctuations and disruptions. DBR therefore can be imple-

Exhibit 2-3
Drum-Buffer-Rope Time Relationships

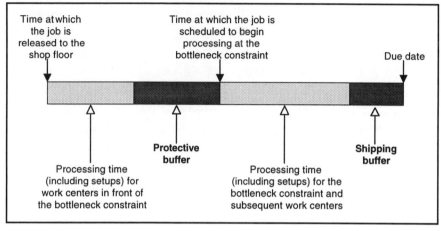

mented much more easily and quickly. In DBR, the schedule is determined by working backwards from the due date of the job. The time at which the job will be scheduled to be loaded onto the bottleneck constraint is determined by subtracting from the due date both the desired size (measured in time) of the shipping buffer and the expected processing time for the bottleneck constraint and all of the subsequent work centers.

The size of the shipping buffer is determined subjectively by balancing the costs of holding finished goods inventories with the consequences of not meeting due dates, taking into account the size and frequency of the delays that normal statistical fluctuations and disruptions can produce. Managers at the DBR sites we visited indicated that some experimentation usually is required to find a comfortable buffer size, but no one seemed bothered by the subjectivity involved in this approach. Most often, managers use a constant shipping buffer expressed as a specified number of days.

The ability to implement DBR without fine-tuning production processes raises an interesting issue. There is a downside to this robustness of DBR. A TOC shop may never get around to improving the operations of the nonconstraints—something that would have to be done for JIT to succeed. Not all improvements in processes yield additional profits. Wringing variation out of processes does not necessarily lead to decreased spending or increased throughput. Nevertheless, the deeper understanding of all processes that comes from careful implementation of JIT may uncover opportunities for real savings that would be overlooked in a DBR implementation.

Returning to the main story, once the time for the job to enter the bottleneck constraint has been scheduled, the release time for the job can be scheduled by allowing for the processing times of the resources in front of the bottleneck constraint and for the desired size of the protective buffer in front of the bottleneck constraint. It is important to note that the sizes of both the shipping and protective buffers are expressed in terms of time. The size of the protective buffer is determined subjectively by balancing the costs of holding work-in-process inventory with the consequences of starving the bottleneck constraint, taking into account the size and frequency of the delays that can (and will) occur because of normal statistical fluctuations and disruptions in the resources in front of the bottleneck constraint. Starving the bottleneck constraint is to be avoided because any time lost on the constraint results in a loss of throughput and hence a reduction of profits.

When an order does not require the use of a bottleneck constraint, it is released to the shop floor according to the due date of the order, taking into account processing times and the desired size of the shipping buffer. In other words, if the shipping buffer is three days, then jobs are released to the shop floor three days earlier than they would be if the plant could be expected to run perfectly with no disruptions. In this case, jobs are pulled through the plant by tying a rope to the due date.

In a DBR system, jobs are released to the shop floor according to the schedule and not before. They then are passed from work center to work center as each work center completes its tasks until the job enters the protective buffer in front of the bottleneck constraint. Because each of the work centers in front of the bottleneck constraint can work at a faster pace than the rate at which work is released into the system, work-in-process inventories in front of the protective buffer ordinarily are minimal. When a job enters the protective buffer, it stays there until the time when it has been scheduled to be loaded onto the bottleneck—and not before. If a job were loaded onto the bottleneck constraint ahead of schedule, it might block another job that was supposed to be using the resource and throw it off schedule. Once a job has been processed by the bottleneck constraint, it is passed on to the next work centers. The job is passed from work center to work center as each work center completes its tasks, just as before. And because the work centers after the bottleneck can work at a faster rate than the bottleneck, the jobs should flow smoothly through the system with very little idle work-in-process.

The companies we visited that were using DBR scheduling reported that very little time or effort was required to set up and run the system. In one case, the DBR system for a plant was designed in less than two days. All of the sites reported dramatic improvements in due date performance, cycle times, and inventory levels, although a few indicated that they had made some mistakes when they were implementing DBR.

Several managers reported to us that it is particularly important to monitor the size of the protective and shipping buffers. Because of normal statistical fluctuations and disruptions, the actual buffers fluctuate in size. The contents of the buffers can provide clues about the health of the system. Managers said that it is particularly important to monitor the protective buffer in front of the bottleneck. "Holes in the protective buffer"—jobs that should be there but aren't—provide an early warning system. For example, if a job has not shown up in the protective buffer on schedule, expediting probably should begin immediately on that job. Expediting at this early point in the process is likely to be much less disruptive and more effective than expediting that occurs only after an irate call from a customer. The Kent Moore system for tracking jobs visually, described in Chapter 4, appeared particularly effective.

Goldratt warns that DBR scheduling commonly clashes with the existing shop floor culture. The desire to measure the performance of individual work centers independent of each other led to elaborate systems of variance reports. This control system both created and required substantial work-in-process inventories. Mackey points out that "a large number of jobs queued up waiting to be worked upon allows department managers to pick and choose among jobs; to match men to machines; to batch together compatible setups, while deferring less suitable jobs.

This strategy, however, creates problems with scheduling production because jobs tend to get lost or delayed, often forcing costly expediting. Traditional accounting provides few incentives to actively reduce these inventories, but rather anticipates excessive inventories so that independent cost-center performance is measurable."[8] [page 197]

According to both JIT and TOC, the cost of being able to measure work center performance independently has been too high. Years of labor efficiency and machine utilization reporting have conditioned everyone to a system in which the apparent objective is to keep everyone and all machines busy all of the time. Because direct labor ordinarily is fixed—at least in the short run—the only way to improve labor efficiency measures such as a standard labor efficiency variance or an hours earned/hours paid ratio is by producing output. Credit is given for anything transferred out of the work center, whether it is sold or not, so performance evaluations based on labor efficiency and machine utilization reports are powerful engines for creating excess work-in-process inventories. The first step in any program aimed at really improving the bottom line must be to turn off such reporting systems—particularly if they are being used to evaluate shop floor performance.

Of course, clerical savings can be realized from shutting down labor efficiency reporting systems. But beyond that, the monthly finger pointing often associated with the variance report can be eliminated. A manager at one site reported that "the production and marketing people used to beat each other up at the monthly meetings over product margins and variances. Under the new system, the focus has changed from the previous attitude of 'not in my cost bucket' to more constructive discussions." Another manager reported that under the old reporting system "we focused on the ratio of direct labor to indirect labor, where the indirect labor included labor time not charged to any job. Everyone knew this, so there was cheating on the time cards to increase the proportion of direct labor. Now we know that some workers *should* be idle in a well-functioning operation."

Even when there is no formal system for reporting efficiencies and utilization rates, most supervisors and managers want to keep everyone and everything busy. This habit must be broken before any progress can be made. "[U]nder no circumstances should we release materials just to supply work to workers. This is probably the most difficult behavior pattern that has to be overcome."[9] Making the transition from a "keep everyone busy" culture to a systems-oriented throughput culture can be difficult for workers as well as for managers and supervisors. "Today if you say: 'Produce only a hundred of these and then thirty of those and then stop,' what do you think will register in the minds of the workers? When was the last time that management told them to stop working? It was five minutes before the layoffs! Every one of the workers will instinctively slow down to prove that you need them."[10]

The temptation to release a job just to keep workers busy can be almost overwhelming but should be resisted. If a job is released prematurely, under the best possible circumstances it will simply show up in the shipping buffer early. However, unscheduled work that is released prematurely is likely to disrupt the schedule and cause other jobs to be late. It is even worse when make-work is created just to keep everyone busy. Make-work generates excess work-in-process and finished goods inventories and almost inevitably will result in deteriorating due date performance and longer cycle times. A manager at one company admitted that in the past they had filled holes in the production schedule by making parts that they hoped they might need someday. This policy resulted in massive piles of work-in-process on the shop floor, which got in the way, took up scarce space, and created major operational problems. Now holes in the production schedule are filled with subcontracting work or not at all.

Managers at several of the sites we visited complained about the persistence of the "keep everyone busy" culture even after management had attempted to explain the logic behind DBR to shop floor personnel. Even after turning off labor efficiency reporting, some supervisors still release jobs prematurely just to keep everyone busy—with predictable negative consequences.

Managers at several companies expressed some concern about the behavioral effects of enforced idleness at nonconstraint work centers. Some believed that workers reacted to disappearing work-in-process inventory by slowing down their pace. These managers were afraid that if workers become accustomed to this more leisurely pace, it might be difficult to pick up the pace later if required. Several managers noted that there were some equity problems between workers at the constraint and at nonconstraints. Workers at nonconstraints may feel less important, have fewer opportunities for overtime, and feel less secure in their jobs.

Most managers we talked to agreed with Goldratt's warning that "the idle time that is an unavoidable result of forcing nonconstraint resources to refrain from overproducing must be filled with something meaningful."[11] At every site we visited where DBR was being used, at least some of the labor had been cross-trained so that individuals could be shifted to the constraint as needed. Also, at most of the sites management had taken pains to explain the DBR system and its implications to employees. Fears about job security in most cases had diminished because of the bottom-line improvements that had resulted from implementation of DBR and TOC techniques. Finally, the amount of enforced idleness at nonconstraints had decreased over time as constraint management techniques improved the flow rate at the bottleneck constraint and disruptions were dealt with more effectively at the nonconstraint work centers. The usual pattern is for an initial decline in work at the nonconstraint work centers as existing work-in-process inventories are liquidated and the system is converted to DBR demand-pull scheduling. Then as processes are improved by managing the bottleneck constraint and dealing with disruptions at nonconstraints, the overall flow rate improves, and there is more work for the nonconstraint work centers.

We do not want to exaggerate the difficulties of dealing with enforced idleness. It is a potential problem to consider when DBR is implemented. Even though some managers were concerned about the possible bad effects of enforced idleness, no one was willing to go back to the old system of make-work just to keep everyone busy.

Managing nonconstraints

When discussing resources that are not constraints in a DBR shop, two cases must be dealt with. The first case is one in which the constraint is outside of the factory. In that situation, all of the factory resources are nonconstraints. The second case is one in which the constraint is inside the factory. In that situation, typically there will be only one constraint and the other resources will be nonconstraints.

In the first case, for a variety of reasons a resource can become a bottleneck temporarily even though theoretically it has enough capacity to meet demand comfortably. The resource itself could break down, the due dates for orders may bunch in such a way that the resource temporarily cannot handle demand, or work centers in front of the resource may suffer disruptions that temporarily dump a glut of work beyond the resource's immediate capacity. All of the sites we visited scheduled resources *as if* the resource with the least capacity relative to current demand was an internal constraint even when the constraint was not currently inside the factory. Managers felt that it was necessary to protect the potential bottleneck with a buffer to prevent it from turning temporarily into a real constraint.

Managers did not ignore the nonconstraints. Indeed, quite a lot of effort went into managing the resources that were not constraints and the protective buffer in front of the constraint. Ideally, the protective buffer will be increased as throughput increases. The reason is that the potential bottleneck constraint is protected by a combination of excess capacity on prior resources and by its protective buffer. As throughput increases, the protective capacity on the prior resources shrinks. To offset this loss of protection, the protective buffer should be increased. If problems hit a resource in front of a potential or real bottleneck constraint, the work stoppage will result in depletion of the protective buffer. If the work stoppage lasts long enough, the protective buffer will be completely consumed, the constraint will be starved, due date delivery performance will suffer, and throughput (and profits) will drop.

Once the underlying cause of the problem is eliminated and the work stoppage ceases, the speed with which the protective buffer can be replenished depends on how much spare capacity is in front of the constraint. If there is little spare capacity, it may take a long time to rebuild the protective buffer. In the meantime, the reduced protective buffer means that less protection from further problems. On the other hand, if the resources in front of the constraint have ample spare capacity, then the protective buffer can replenished fairly quickly. The optimal buffer size in front of a potential or real constraint depends on how much spare capacity the prior resources have. This capacity in turn depends on the product mix and overall volume, so ideally the protective time buffer should be dynamically adjusted.

Simple manual DBR systems with fixed protective buffers compensate for fluctuating market demand by inflating the protective buffer and by using overtime to rebuild protective buffers when there are serious disruptions. More complex DBR systems with dynamic buffering require sophisticated software and the power of a computer. Dynamic buffering, along with scheduling, "what if" modeling, and other features, is incorporated in the curiously named software Disaster, which has been developed by the Avraham Y. Goldratt Institute. The basic logic of this program is explained in *The Haystack Syndrome*. We did not visit any site that was using a released version of this software, although several sites were involved in testing pre-release versions. The AGI advises clients that they really need this software only if their constraint is inside the plant and they have little protective capacity on the nonconstraint resources.

In addition to adjusting the protective buffers to volume and the product mix, managers also can strive to reduce disruptions that threaten throughput. By carefully monitoring the locations of the jobs that are late in arriving at the buffers it may be possible to identify where the disruptions usually occur. Once the source of the disruptions has been identified, the specific causes of the disruptions can be addressed. For example, the cause may be frequent machine breakdowns on a particular machine. In this case, preventive maintenance efforts should be focused on this machine. Or the disruptions could be caused by a policy that dictates large batches on a particular piece of equipment. In this case, supervisors can be directed to reduce the batch sizes. (See the Company J case in the next chapter for an example.) If it is difficult to pinpoint the causes of the disruptions, quality control techniques from TQM can be invaluable. These techniques work by stabilizing and improving processes so that there is very little variation. They are well suited to the task of removing disruptions in the process.

With regard to TQM, Goldratt asserts that the results of TQM have been mixed because TQM has not been focused on the areas where improvements can have the greatest effects—on the system's constraints. This fact often has led to local improvement in processes without any discernible bottom-line effect. Very few of the sites we visited were involved heavily in TQM. However, where such improvement programs were in place, opinion was unanimous that there are synergies between TOC and TQM. TOC helps identify where TQM tools should be focused. One person stated, "Essentially, JIT improves lead times and due date performance, TQM improves people, and TOC provides focus for the entire improvement process."

Managing constraints—the process of ongoing improvement

Thus far, the discussion has centered on ways to manage around the constraint. That is, the existence of the constraint is taken as a given and the problem is to figure out how to optimize within the limitations it imposes. However, TOC does not stop there. As Tom Johnson has pointed out, managers who want to make real progress must learn to break the constraints rather than just accept them.[12] This insight is reflected in the five focusing steps for ongoing improvement that were introduced in *The Goal* and are reproduced in Exhibit 2-4. By successfully following the five steps, and particularly by not allowing inertia to set in, an organization can break one constraint after another and keep moving forward. This sounds wonderful in theory, but how is it actually done?

Exhibit 2-4
The Process of Ongoing Improvement

Step 1. Identify the system's constraint(s).
Step 2. Decide how to exploit the system's constraint(s).
Step 3. Subordinate everything else to the above decision.
Step 4. Elevate the constraint(s).
Step 5. If a constraint has been broken, go back to Step 1. Do not allow
        inertia to cause a system constraint.

Step 1. Identify the system's constraint(s)

In a well-run factory, the constraint can be identified easily by the location of work-in-process inventories. If the factory is well managed, they will be concentrated in front of the constraint. In a poorly run factory, work-in-process inventories will be scattered all over, and identification of the real constraint is initially more difficult.

At several sites managers told us that they had been unable to figure out where the bottleneck was because of the chaos that had resulted from applying conventional shop control techniques over the years. Rather than giving up, they picked a resource near the middle of the system to be the "designated constraint" and then proceeded to install a DBR system. This procedure permitted some progress in getting the production process under control. If the initial guess at the location of the constraint was incorrect, the system eventually would let them know by the presence of unplanned work-in-process inventory accumulating in front of the real constraint and perhaps by holes in the protective buffer in front of the "designated constraint."

Goldratt believes that the physical constraints on the shop floor usually can be dealt with very quickly once they have been identified. As soon as the constraints inside the factory have been broken, the constraint shifts elsewhere. Quite often it will appear that the market is the constraint—there is insufficient demand for the company's products. In such a situation, it appears that the constraint is outside of the company and therefore beyond its control. However, Goldratt firmly believes that in the vast majority of cases, the real constraint is some policy inside the company. "We very rarely find a company with a real market constraint, but rather, with devastating marketing policy constraints."[13] For example, a company may have a policy of never cutting its prices below its fully allocated product costs.

Unfortunately, it can be extraordinarily difficult to identify a policy constraint. Most such constraints are unwritten and often unverbalized rules that everyone follows without thinking. Quite often, these policies exist for reasons that no one can remember. The Current Reality Tree, which is one of the techniques used in the Thinking Process, was designed explicitly to identify such policy constraints. We will discuss the Current Reality Tree later in this chapter. When a constraint is a policy, it should be replaced with a better policy. In that case, steps 2 and 3 in the Process of Ongoing Improvement should be skipped.

Step 2. Decide how to exploit the system's constraint(s)

In the exploitation step, the idea is not to waste any of the constrained resource. For example, defective units destined for the scrap heap should be removed from the work flow before they go through the constraint—not after. Labor can be added to the constraint to ensure that it is kept operating during normal breaks and shift changes. The constraint can be "overstaffed" to help reduce lost time due to setups, and routine maintenance can be done after normal working hours. At the sites we visited we found a large number of examples of such simple steps that reduce wasted time on the constraint and therefore increase throughput.

Potential jobs also should be prioritized in terms of how effectively they use the constrained resource. The constraint is wasted if it is used to process one job when a different job could have produced more profit. Such decisions can be made by prioritizing potential jobs according to the amount of throughput they yield per unit of the constrained resource. (This method is exactly the same as prioritizing products based on the contribution margin per unit of the constraint, which has been included as a constraint management technique in management accounting textbooks for decades.)

More subtly, companies can use pricing to ensure an adequate return for the use of the constraint. We found several companies using pricing in this way.

Step 3. Subordinate everything else to the above decision

Subordination defines the role of nonconstraint operations. The purpose is to protect the set of decisions regarding exploiting the constraint during day-to-day operations. The clearest example of subordination is provided by the DBR scheduling system in which the constraint sets the pace for the entire system. Another example is the use of utilization and efficiency measures for the constraint that focus plantwide efforts on maximizing throughput.

This is a major shift for management accounting. Caspari stated it clearly when he wrote, "The question becomes: What must this unconstrained area do to protect the exploitation decisions? rather than: What can this area do by itself to increase the bottom line?"[14] The obvious conclusion is that nonconstraints should be measured on how well they support the constraint and definitely not on local "cost" minimization actions. Any decision regarding nonconstrained resources needs to be answered in light of how the action will involve or impact the constraint. The focus is on throughput maximization, not cost minimization.

Goldratt warns:

> So many times we have witnessed a situation where everybody was complaining about a huge constraint, but when they exercised the second step of exploitation, of just not wasting what was available, it turned out that there was more than enough. So let's not hastily run to approve subcontracting, or launch a fancy new advertising campaign, etc. When the second and third steps are complete and we still have a constraint, that is the time to move to the fourth step. . . .[15]

For example, the constraint at one site was space, and plans had been made to expand the size of the plant. The response was to reorganize production lines, cut batch sizes, and reduce setup times. These actions reduced the size of WIP and therefore reduced storage space requirements. Production doubled, cycle time was reduced to three days from 10, and WIP was cut by 80%. The space saved by reconfiguring production lines and reducing inventories resulted in shelving the plans to expand the plant.

Step 4. Elevate the system's constraint(s)

Elevating the constraint means getting more of it. Some of the work that ordinarily would go through the bottleneck constraint might be off-loaded to outside shops. If the bottleneck is a machine, another can be acquired. At most of the sites we visited, recent equipment acquisitions had focused on elevating the constraint. We found several examples in which very inexpensive used equipment with limited capabilities was used to off-load some of the work from a constraint. Ordinarily, this equipment would have been cast off as too inefficient to use. Overtime, or even another shift, often was used to add capacity to the constraint. At one site, the standard product used a bottleneck, but the premium product did not. Managers decided to give free upgrades to the premium product. This decision never would have been made under their old operating rules, which emphasized "cost" minimization, because the premium product requires more total machine time (but on the nonbottlenecks) than the standard product and hence is more "expensive." Almost every site we visited had been able to increase the overall capacity of the plant by effective constraint management, to the point where throughput ordinarily was no longer limited by the capacity of the plant. The constraint had shifted outside of the plant to the market or to some other part of the organization.

Step 5. If a constraint has been broken, go back to Step 1. Do not allow inertia to be the new system constraint

If a constraint has been broken, something else immediately will become the constraint. Energies and attention then must shift to identifying and dealing effectively with that new constraint. Policies established to support the old constraint must be changed or eliminated. If this process does not occur, progress will stop and likely will even be reversed as disillusionment sets in.

The story we were told at one site reinforces the importance of overcoming inertia. The organization had substantial initial successes with TOC, but stagnation set in because of a change in constraints. Because of a dramatic shift in demand toward more complex products, the constraint had shifted to product engineering. The shift created a number of problems, including a tendency for jobs to be released by engineering in big bursts that would overwhelm the productive capacity of the plant. There had been no visible attempt to overcome this problem using TOC principles. It did not even seem to occur to managers to use TOC principles to attack the problem. Such a situation probably is a consequence of the tendency to view TOC as a set of tools for production and not as more generalized tools that can be applied to engineering, marketing, or other nonmanufacturing functions.

This last example notwithstanding, we were told consistently that the focus on constraints in TOC was perhaps its greatest contribution. One manager said, "TOC is common sense, but TOC is *not* common practice. We knew the benefits of focusing on the constraints all along, but in practice we were looking everywhere." Another manager said, "We used to spend 80% of our time dealing with unimportant issues that seemed important at the time. Now we spend 80% of our time on the core problems."

The Thinking Process—an overview

TOC usually is introduced into an organization as a result of someone's reading *The Goal.* Because the book is about a production manager in a job shop that is having difficulty filling orders on time, TOC tends to be applied first to just such situations, where the applications are most obvious. That is, TOC usually is applied first by production managers in a job shop experiencing the problems encountered in *The Goal*. The results of our interviews with managers indicate that improvements in such settings can be very rapid and dramatic, and initially these improvements result in higher profits. However, continual improvement in the production area eventually leads to excess productive capacity without any profit improvement. The constraint shifts outside of the factory. Most frequently the new constraint is a policy constraint rather than a physical constraint. That is, some policy prevents the company from increasing its profits. This is even true of situations in which the constraint seems to be insufficient demand; the real problem is likely to be some policy that prevents aggressive exploitation of market opportunities. Policies are often responses to problems that occurred long ago, and they often are accepted and followed without thinking. Such policies may be unwritten and just "part of the woodwork." Policy constraints can be quite difficult to identify, and once identified, they can be very difficult to elevate. Quite often, elevating policy constraints requires cooperation across departmental boundaries.

While the Thinking Process can be used to tackle physical as well as policy constraints, it is particularly valuable when dealing with the latter. The Thinking Process begins with the premise that to improve, people need to be able to answer three questions: "What to change?" "What to change to?" and "How to change?" The Thinking Process consists of formal analytical tools that are intended to help people answer these three questions. The roles played by the tools are summarized in Exhibit 2-5. A specific problem may require the use of all of the tools, but they also can be used selectively.

Exhibit 2-5
The Roles of the Thinking Process Tools

What to change?	What to change to?	How to change?
Current Reality Tree	Evaporating Cloud	Prerequisite Tree
	Future Reality Tree	Transition Tree

The Current Reality Tree is used to diagnose causes or "core problems." As in medicine, a diagnosis begins with a list of symptoms. In the Thinking Process the symptoms are called "Undesirable Effects," or UDEs. (UDE is pronounced you-dee.) Based on the pattern of observed symptoms, a common cause is deduced. Up to a point, the more symptoms there are, the easier it is to make the diagnosis. A single symptom can have many causes, but a pattern of different symptoms may have only a single plausible cause. Rather than relying entirely on intuition to find the cause, a formal cause-and-effect map (Current Reality Tree) is constructed with the objective of identifying a few core problems that can explain all (or virtually all) of the observed Undesirable Effects.

An underlying assumption in the Thinking Process is that almost all of the Undesirable Effects in any organization have a common cause. In practice, we found that when the original list of Undesirable Effects drawn up by a manager was large and consisted of seemingly unrelated effects, the "core problem" often would turn out to be vague and general. In such cases, the core problem usually was identified as some variation on the theme "we don't have well-defined, effective policies." However, when the list of Undesirable Effects was relatively small and more obviously related, the core problem was usually much more concrete and specific. The reason for this phenomenon is fairly evident. If almost all of the Undesirable Effects must be linked to some core problem and the Undesirable Effects are barely related, then the core problem must be something very broad and nonspecific such as "we don't have well-defined, effective policies."

Once a core problem has been identified using intuition or a Current Reality Tree, the question becomes "What to change to?" The initial statement of the solution, or objective, is usually just the opposite of the core problem. So if the core problem is "we do not have enough sales in the winter," then the objective becomes "we have enough sales in the winter." Sometimes stating the objective is sufficient—the steps to be taken to arrive at the solution are obvious intuitively. However, as in this example, the means of obtaining the objective may be far from obvious. If there were some easy way to increase sales in the winter, presumably something would have been done already.

The persistence of a core problem often indicates that there is some conflict that blocks its resolution. That is, the lack of sales in the winter may not be due to a lack of effort but to some unresolved conflict. For example, it may be due to a conflict between the desire to keep prices up to protect normal margins and a desire to cut prices to increase unit volume. In such situations, compromise solutions are common. Prices may be cut a bit in winter but not enough to seriously erode normal margins. Goldratt rejects such compromise solutions and believes that a solution not requiring any compromise is almost always available. The key is to identify the assumptions that lead us to *believe* that a clean solution is not possible. The specific technique used to identify the assumptions underlying the apparent conflict and to break the deadlock is called an "Evaporating Cloud."[16] In the simple example, the hidden assumption may be that it is necessary to drop prices in existing markets to increase sales in the winter. However, a better approach might be to enter an entirely new market in the winter. This more concrete objective would become the "injection" around which a solution would be built.

Several examples of the use of the Evaporating Cloud technique from our field investigations are included in the next chapter. It appears to us that the technique can be a valuable way to verbalize conflicts that may be preventing a successful solution to a current core problem. By verbalizing these conflicts and the assumptions underlying them, breakthrough solutions are more likely.

Goldratt believes that it is always possible to evaporate a cloud (i.e., find a way to obtain the objective without compromising), but we are skeptical. Nevertheless, the Jonah training course gives many examples of the use of Evaporating Clouds to achieve breakthrough solutions to apparently intractable problems. These examples, together with Goldratt's insistence that there is always a way to evaporate the cloud, give some people the willpower to press onwards even though they might have thrown up their hands and compromised before.

Several Jonahs said that the Evaporating Cloud technique has proved to be the most valuable part of their training and has been of decisive importance in business situations. In fact, some of the Jonahs we interviewed said that they seldom take the trouble to build Current Reality Trees; they believe they can identify core problems quite readily on the fly. However, they said that they frequently use Evaporating Clouds to brainstorm solutions.

Once an injection (the basis of a solution) has been identified, a Future Reality Tree is used to check whether successful implementation of the injection will eliminate the symptoms. It also is used to check whether the injection is likely to generate new negative consequences. If the injection is insufficient to eliminate the symptoms or if the injection itself would have negative consequences, the solution is modified—perhaps using another Evaporating Cloud. The process of refining the solution continues until the preparer is confident that successful implementation of the solution will eliminate a significant portion of the original symptoms without leading to new, even worse negative consequences.

Next the question becomes, How to cause the change? All of the imaginable obstacles to implementing the injection are laid out in the Prerequisite Tree. The final tool, the Transition Tree, identifies the specific actions that should be taken to overcome the obstacles identified in the Prerequisite Tree. Essentially, the Transition Tree is the implementation plan.

We have given a very quick overview of a subject that is complex and involves unfamiliar terms. As mentioned earlier, the Appendix on the Thinking Process contains more details and can serve as a simple tutorial on the basics of the Thinking Process.

The Thinking Process—our evaluation

Goldratt claims that the Thinking Process can be used to develop a successful plan to deal with *any* organizational, personal, or interpersonal problem that can be solved. The magnitude of this claim is astonishing. However, it should not be dismissed too lightly. The Thinking Process appears to be an elaborate logical system, that is, a system for understanding and manipulating cause-and-effect relationships.

Some people would claim that the most interesting and important problems are not amenable to logical analysis, and therefore any approach based on logic is doomed to failure.[17] We have no desire to become mired in deep philosophical discussions about the practical limits of logic. However, to the extent that problems have causes, it seems to us that some sort of logical system is required if one intends to deal effectively with problems.

Having said that, we must admit that we don't know whether the Thinking Process is really a coherent logical system. Does it obey basic laws of logic such as internal consistency? Are there gaps in the logic anywhere? We simply don't know, although there are no obvious errors or omissions in the procedures. Our impression is that the Thinking Process could be a breakthrough in the application of logic to practical problem solving, but then we are not professional logicians.

On the other hand, we did talk to a lot of people who had received training of one sort or another in the Thinking Process. There were very few sites at which all of the steps in the Thinking Process were being used regularly—and even then, there were few instances in which the entire Thinking Process, from Current Reality Tree to Transition Tree, was used to attack a problem. Moreover, most of the Jonahs we interviewed had not used the Thinking Process to any significant extent except during the Jonah course itself.

They expressed some guilt about their failure to use the Thinking Process. Nearly everyone felt that the results are very good when the tools are used, but most of them felt that their training in the Thinking Process had been inadequate and that building trees is too time consuming. These complaints are interrelated. Through regular practice, proficiency in the Thinking Process improves, and it becomes much easier and quicker to build trees. However, those who felt that their Jonah training was inadequate do not have the confidence to use the tools on a regular basis and therefore do not improve their skills to the point where the benefit they gain seems to be worth all the effort.

Does this infrequent use of the Thinking Process mean that it is a bust? We don't think so—for several reasons. First, portions of the Thinking Process were being used on a regular basis in about a third of the sites we visited. At these sites we saw some apparently very successful applications of tools from the Thinking Process. Some of these applications are documented in the next chapter.

Second, we believe it is premature to judge the success or failure of the Thinking Process. It simply has not been around long enough for us to come to any firm conclusions. It has been evolving since about 1987 and was still undergoing revision while this book was being written. As the Thinking Process was developed, it was introduced slowly into the Jonah course curriculum. The first elements— Current Reality Trees and Evaporating Clouds—were introduced into the Jonah course only in 1988. The first version of the Jonah course to concentrate mainly on the Thinking Process rather than on production management was offered in 1991. That course generally is acknowledged by all concerned to have been a disaster. Unfortunately, quite a few of the Jonahs we interviewed had attended that particular version of the course. The "standard" version of the Jonah course, which now is devoted almost entirely to the Thinking Process, was introduced only in 1992. It has been undergoing revision ever since. All of our contacts for interviewing came from attending two Jonah conferences—one held in October 1992 and the other in

February 1993. Very few people at those conferences had taken the Jonah course recently enough to have been trained in the whole Thinking Process.

We encountered various uses of the Thinking Process that give some idea of the range of issues it can deal with. At one site, Current Reality Trees were used to diagnose problems with meeting production schedules and with failures in the product design and development process. At another site, Current Reality Trees were used to address problems with low profits, with failed improvement programs, with poor management information systems, and with vendors. At another site, a Future Reality Tree was used in a decision to build a new facility.

Managers at one location used Evaporating Clouds to find injections for the objectives "customers want to buy from a single vendor (us)" and "the customer will want to buy in smaller quantities." Current Reality Trees at the same site dealt with poor interactions among divisions and with a financial crisis. At another site, Current Reality Trees dealt with inadequate cash flow and working capital problems, difficulties associated with seasonal sales patterns, and large overtime expenses. At the same site, Evaporating Clouds had as their objectives a better system for motivating salespersons and increasing profits without increasing volume. Future Reality Trees at the company had as their objectives a new performance measurement system and better coordination among departments. A Transition Tree was built to clear up production problems. At another site, Current Reality Trees focused on problems with customers being put on hold on the telephone and poor due date performance. At another site, an Evaporating Cloud dealt with the conflict between forcing people to use the Thinking Process and letting them invent solutions their own way, and so on.

At some sites, attempts had been made to build trees as a group. The results were decidedly mixed. Some managers said that their experience with building consensus trees was fabulous. We heard comments such as "meetings used to be a big waste of time. Now we really get something done." Managers who used this technique to structure meetings claimed that "buy-in" was almost guaranteed. Some of these managers said that the technique even worked with non-Jonahs in the group. There was one site where the standard procedure at the annual management retreat was to build a Current Reality Tree based on all of the managers' lists of current Undesirable Effects. One manager said he uses trees to structure meetings that tackle especially tough problems. As an example, he said trees were used in a general management meeting to decide whether to lay off employees. The trees forced people to focus on understanding the problem and how their actions affect the entire organization.

At other sites, however, managers said they had tried to build trees in a group setting and the effort was a complete flop. The reasons given were "finger-pointing" and too much variance in individuals' abilities to create and understand trees. There were also instances in which building trees in groups did not work because the rules for building trees—in particular, the categories of legitimate reservations—were not followed. We do not have any explanation for why consensus trees seem to work in some companies and not in others. The explanation certainly is not educational level. If anything, there was a negative correlation between the educational attainments of group members and the success of consensus trees.

Quite a few managers commented that some people take more naturally to the Thinking Process than others. Not surprisingly, the Thinking Process was said to appeal more to analytical than to intuitive thinkers. At one company there was even some worry that if the Thinking Process became too entrenched, less analytical managers might be driven out of the company. The president of this company, who was not a Jonah, felt that successful marketing managers in particular would feel uncomfortable with the Thinking Process. We certainly met very few Jonahs who are in marketing, which could be due simply to the fact that most companies become interested in

TOC as a result of reading *The Goal.* As a consequence, TOC is widely perceived to be "a production thing." The Avraham Y. Goldratt Institute currently is running seminars specifically for marketing people, but we did not talk to anyone who had taken this course.

At some sites, trees were used as devices for communicating with people who have no familiarity with the Thinking Process. Trees compactly describe chains of reasoning that can be quite complex and that would take far longer to explain with conventional text. At one company, the production manager used trees to convince the president of the company that he should abandon his hiring freeze and hire more people. At another company, trees were used to explain a major facility expansion to the board of directors and to bankers. A manager at another site offered the following advice:

> If people ask what the Thinking Process is, don't answer—there is no satisfactory short answer. You will leave the impression of a lunatic if you try. Instead, start with your Current Reality Tree from the bottom up and they will give you all the time you need. We have learned that there is nothing more persuasive and convincing than trees written by the people who work in the company on the problems of the company.

The Thinking Process—summary

The Thinking Process is an intriguing collection of logic-based tools that promises to help people diagnose problems, find solutions, and draw up successful implementation plans. It is quite general and can be applied to many kinds of problems from the shop floor to the executive suite. However, it is not infallible. Bad decisions can be made using the Thinking Process—we observed a few. Like any other decision process, the Thinking Process relies on the quality of the information brought to it. It does seem, however, to be very well thought out and to offer numerous checks that serve to minimize decision-making errors.

In practice, very few of the people who had been trained in the Thinking Process actually were using it routinely, possibly because it is a recent development and very few of the people we interviewed felt their training had been adequate. Despite the disappointing low general usage, we did find some companies that used the Thinking Process extensively and routinely, and we found numerous examples of occasional use. People who have used elements of the Thinking Process almost unanimously say the elements have been very valuable. For most people, the Thinking Process seems to be like physical exercise—something you avoid doing, but once you have done it you are glad you did. It forces discipline in decisions and can yield important new insights. In a group setting it can be used to build consensus and to elicit information efficiently from individuals. The Thinking Process provides a comprehensive set of articulated tools for diagnosing problems and designing actionable solutions.

Notes

1. Eliyahu M. Goldratt and Robert E. Fox, *The Race*, 1986, North River Press, Croton-on-Hudson, N.Y., p. 60.

2. Of course, full costing is not the only reason excessive work-in-process inventories are built. In traditional job shops, work-in-process inventories between work centers serve to decouple them and allow them to be run more independently. And as discussed later, the emphasis in traditional shops on "efficiency" and reducing unit costs also leads to building inventories.

3. Goldratt uses the term "inventories" to refer to what accountants call "assets." We will ignore this idiosyncrasy and simply use the term assets. Goldratt never mentions liabilities, so apparently he is satisfied with the way liabilities are measured by accountants. Indeed, he seems to take no notice of the balance sheet at all. In Throughput Accounting, assets are used only as the denominator in the return on assets.

4. Eliyahu M. Goldratt, *The Haystack Syndrome: Sifting Information Out of the Data Ocean*, 1990, North River Press, Croton-on-Hudson, N.Y., pp. 20 & 22.

5. Eliyahu M. Goldratt & Robert E. Fox, *The Theory of Constraints Journal*, Volume 1, Number 4, February/March 1989, pp. 10-11.

6. Some cautionary notes have begun to appear in the accounting literature concerning the relevance of ABC data in decisions. See, for example, Alfred M. King, "Green Dollars and Blue Dollars: The Paradox of Cost Reduction," *Journal of Cost Management*, Fall 1993, pp. 44-52.

7. Goldratt, *The Haystack Syndrome*, op. cit.

8. James Mackey, "Chapter 10: MRP, JIT and automated manufacturing and the role of the accountant in production management," in *Issues in Management Accounting*, edited by David Ashton, Trevor Hopper, and Robert W. Scapens, Prentice Hall, Hertfordshire, Great Britain, 1991, pp. 193-218.

9. Goldratt and Fox, *The Race*, op. cit., p. 114.

10. Goldratt, *The Haystack Syndrome*, op. cit., pp. 87-88.

11. Ibid., p. 89.

12. H. Thomas Johnson, "Professors, Customers, and Value: Bringing a Global Perspective to Management Accounting Education," *Performance Excellence in Manufacturing and Service Organizations*, edited by Peter B.B. Turney, Proceedings of the Third Annual Management Accounting Symposium, San Diego, Cal., March 1989, American Accounting Association, 1990, p. 19.

13. Eliyahu M. Goldratt, *The Theory of Constraints*, North River Press, Croton-on-Hudson, N.Y., p. 6.

14. John Caspari, in *Management Accountants' Handbook*, fourth edition, 1994 cumulative supplement, Donald E. Keller, James Bulloch, and Robert L. Shultis, eds., John Wiley & Sons, New York, 1994.

15. Goldratt, *The Haystack Syndrome*, op. cit., p. 61.

16. Shigeo Shingo suggests a similar logical process for breaking deadlocks based on the dialectical method. Like Goldratt, he rejects compro-

mise solutions and advocates breaking the assumptions underlying the apparent conflict. He also suggests the rudiments of a Drum-Buffer-Rope shop control system. Shingo and Goldratt appear to be thinking along very similar lines, although Shingo tends to stress the detailed tactics of improvement such as setup time and defect reduction whereas Goldratt tends to stress the strategic aspects of where to focus the improvement efforts. See Shigeo Shingo and Alan Robinson, *Modern Approaches to Manufacturing Improvement: The Shingo System*, Productivity Press, Cambridge, Mass., 1990, especially pages 29-30 and 155.

17. It is interesting to note that the Thinking Process already is being used by at least one psychologist to help people deal with their personal problems.

3 Case Studies _____

Introduction

This chapter provides details of how specific companies are using TOC in their day-to-day operations and strategy. The seven companies discussed here were the most interesting and, by-and-large, the most successful TOC sites we visited. A wide variety of TOC techniques and tools were being used, from Drum-Buffer-Rope scheduling to the use of the Thinking Process in planning and presenting major plant expansions. Four of the seven companies are located in Europe. All are involved in manufacturing and most are job shops. Two of the sites are subsidiaries of large multinational corporations; the remainder of the companies are privately held and had at most several hundred employees. Two of the companies requested that we disguise their identity because of the sensitivity of some of the information. These companies are identified as Company J and Company Q in this chapter. In a few instances data were disguised in the write-ups of other companies. These instances are indicated clearly in the relevant exhibits.

We are indebted to the managers at Baxter, Hofmans Forms Packing, Kent Moore Cabinets, Samsonite Europe, and Western Textile Products in addition to the managers of Company J and Company Q for providing us access and permitting us to publish the following information.

61

Baxter—Lessines, Belgium

Baxter Corporation is a multinational company involved in health care products. The Lessines plant, located in the French-speaking part of Belgium, employs about 900 people and has been in operation since 1970. The plant produces sterile plastic bags for intravenous solutions, peritoneal dialysis bags, and plastic parts. Nearly everything made at Lessines is transferred to other Baxter subsidiaries rather than being sold to outside customers.

In 1988 the production of examination gloves, which was about half of Lessines' total volume, was shut down. The latex gloves production was moved to Malaysia to be near the source of the latex raw material. The production of vinyl gloves was discontinued as vinyl gloves were no longer a viable, cost-effective alternative to latex gloves. More than 300 people were laid off, and the equipment for making gloves was scrapped, creating a crisis situation.

The general manager, Max Bataille, and his assistant, Emmanuel Amory, have been involved in TOC since 1989 and both are Jonahs. Bataille reports:

> Our experience with TOC has been a saga. It is not easy. It has been a four-year saga from the first encounter involving a lot of mistakes, a lot of fights, overzealousness, communication problems, and resistance. But there are rewards also. Despite losing half of the plant's volume at one fell swoop four years ago due to an external event, the plant is now running at capacity, operating expense is down despite a more diverse and complex product line, service is up, and our unit costs—which are the prices we charge our customers—are down by double digit percentages.

The Lessines plant is unique in this study because it is thriving in an environment in which its performance is evaluated based on standard cost variances—with an important twist. Instead of being evaluated on the detailed cost variance report, higher management at Baxter has agreed to evaluate Lessines based on the total overall variance. Thus, the Lessines general manager can choose to take an action that will result in an unfavorable variance providing that it is offset by a favorable variance elsewhere.

While the detailed variance report is complex, when viewed as a whole it is fairly simple. The overall total variance is basically the difference between the plant's output evaluated at full absorption standard product costs and the plant's actual costs. (The full absorption standard product costs are set annually based on budgeted costs and volumes.) Essentially, the general manager is evaluated as if the plant were a profit center, with output prices being the full absorption standard product costs.

Because the Lessines general manager is evaluated based on what is essentially a profit calculation, he can apply the usual TOC analysis to his situation. By aggressively seeking new business within the company, he can get more orders and then use TOC techniques to squeeze more throughput (i.e., volume) out of the system. All other things being equal, if the plant produces more volume than was budgeted, the overall variance will be favorable. In the detailed variance report, the increase in throughput shows up as a favorable volume variance. Lessines can "sell" the increased volume to other divisions because of its lower average cost (which results in lower transfer prices) and improved quality.

The shift in thinking is profound. Instead of being a cost center evaluated based on the minute details of a cost variance report, the plant is for all practical purposes a profit center. Instead of minimizing unit costs, the plant strives to maximize its profit, which is its actual throughput (evaluated using the frozen full absorption standard product costs) less its actual operating expenses. This goal changes the orientation of the plant toward satisfying the customer (i.e., other divisions) to get more business and away from the relatively sterile orientation of cost minimization. The irony is that this change in orientation actually has decreased the cost to the customer at the same time that profit has increased and quality has gone up.

The reason for this paradox is that the old detailed variance reporting system assumes that minimizing unit costs everywhere in the system will minimize unit costs for the whole system. In fact, the attempt to minimize unit cost everywhere leads to higher, not lower, global unit costs. Among other things, attempting to minimize unit costs at each work station frequently results in mountains of excess work-in-process inventories.

The difference in orientation between being evaluated on the basis of detailed standard cost variances and being evaluated based on the overall total variance is illustrated with an actual situation from Lessines. A rough flowchart for the sterile bag production line is displayed in Exhibit 3-1. Raw plastic pellets are blended for desired

Exhibit 3-1
Sterile Bag Fabrication

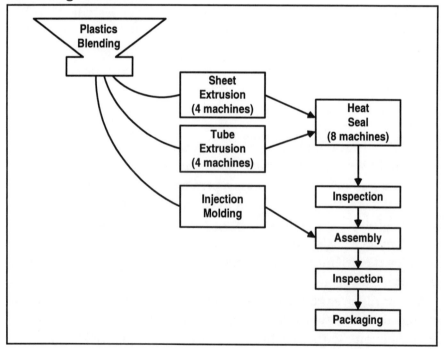

properties and then are sent to one of three processes: sheet extrusion, tube extrusion, or injection molding. Extruded sheets and tubes are sealed together in heat sealing to form unfinished bags. The bags then pass on to assembly where various parts are added. For purposes of this illustration it is important to note that the heat sealers are not identical—they have different capabilities—and a variety of different products are fabricated in this process.

At one point, two of the eight heat sealers in plastics fabrication were the constraint in the process. These two heat sealers (call them machines A and B) were uniquely suited to processing five products, and they just couldn't keep up with demand. One of these products (call it product 5) could be off-loaded to another less efficient but underutilized heat sealer (call it machine C). Because overhead is distributed based on machine time and the standard machine time for product 5 assumes that machine A or B will be used for processing, off-loading product 5 onto a less efficient machine would result in unfavorable overhead variances.

In addition, more scrap is generated on machine C than on machine A or B. Because the materials quantity standard for the product assumes that machine A or B will be used, running product 5 on machine C would result in an unfavorable material usage variance.

Another way to deal with the heat sealer bottleneck would be to double the manning on machines A and B. However, it would result in unfavorable labor efficiency variances.

It is true that these unfavorable variances would be offset by a favorable volume variance, but this favorable effect may not attract as much attention in the typical review of manufacturing performance as the unfavorable variances. As a result, in a conventional standard cost variance reporting environment managers may be reluctant to elevate a constraint by using "less efficient" methods.

In contrast, the TOC approach clearly indicated that both offloading and double manning were fully justified. The increase in throughput exceeded the increase in operating expenses, and inventories or other assets did not change significantly.[1] Therefore, the actions generated a favorable overall variance. In general, Lessines management feels that actions should be evaluated based on their impacts on throughput, operating expenses, and assets. While the vocabulary they use is a bit different, the approach is quite similar to the relevant cost approach to evaluating alternatives that is taught in management accounting textbooks.

The third step in the five-step procedure for managing constraints is to subordinate everything else to the constraint. Sheet extruders were feeding the heat sealers constraint, but materials were being run through the sheet extruders in large batches to minimize setup times. It is important to note that some of the output of the sheet extruders goes through the bottleneck heat sealers, but some also goes through heat sealers that are not bottlenecks. Thus, because of the large batch sizes, the sheet extruders might be run for long periods processing materials that don't go through the bottleneck. During this period the work-in-process buffers in front of the bottlenecks might run dry, and thus the bottleneck would be starved. Therefore, the batch sizes on the sheet extruders were reduced. However, in a conventional, tightly controlled cost variance reporting system this action would have resulted in unfavorable variances on the extruders due to more setups.

Returning to the main story, how did the Lessines plant manage to recover from the 50% drop in volume in 1988? Using TOC and other techniques, the plant was able to lower its costs (and therefore its transfer prices), increase its quality, and improve its on-time delivery. As a consequence, Lessines received more orders from the other divisions of Baxter.

Bataille emphasizes that one of the big benefits of TOC is that it gives them the courage to go above 85% of capacity—a utilization rate that former management had regarded as an upper practical limit. Indeed, former management had turned down business rather than go above the 85% limit. With TOC they understand and can control the process much better, so they are now able to operate routinely at 95%+ of capacity. With TOC, they know what to expect, and they know how to manage the process so they won't get into trouble.

Part of this control comes from using a manual Drum-Buffer-Rope (DBR) approach to scheduling. Over a four-year period cycle times were reduced from five days to half a day in one product line and from 35 days to three days in another. The benefits of DBR, apart from reduced cycle times, are protection of throughput, low inventories, reduced traffic flows, better buffer management, and a clearer management process.

Management of the plant takes a very proactive stance toward managing the bottlenecks. When materials are a constraint, they may go to a secondary vendor and purchase the materials at a higher cost than normal. When a machine is the constraint, it may be elevated temporarily by manning it with an added weekend shift. When asked about the floating bottleneck problem, management responded that the bottleneck constraints do change, but the changes are planned. TOC helps predict where constraints will be. With long lead times for acquiring machines, capacity can be added where and when it is needed. For example, a new extruding machine is about to be installed that will elevate the current constraint. When that machine is up and running, the constraint is expected to shift to the blenders; a new blender is already planned.

Occasionally, a policy is the real constraint. For example, it appeared that there wasn't enough plastic sheeting, a raw material, to satisfy demand. Upon investigation, management found that plastic sheeting was being routed to a central warehouse where it would sit for up to 50 days before enough of it accumulated to be used in large-scale batch production. "We were in love with big homogeneous batches." To break this bottleneck, management routed the plastic sheeting directly to the factory where it was used in smaller batches. This change eliminated four positions involved in moving sheeting back and forth, reduced inventory from a 50-day supply to a six-day supply, and increased throughput.

Lessines' management has used formal trees to structure meetings that tackle tough problems—particularly those involving personnel. Management's experience is that without the trees, nothing much is accomplished in such meetings. Using the Thinking Process (TP) in meetings forces people to focus on understanding a problem and how their actions affect others and the entire organization. Trees are invaluable in getting buy-in from others—even those with no training in the Thinking Process.

Lessines was one of the few sites in our study that was actively involved in TQM. Lessines management believes that TOC and TQM are complementary tools. TOC focuses the quality improvement effort where it can really make a difference. Which projects should be tackled today? Where should we work on scrap reduction? TOC provides the answers.

Bataille summed up his views about one of the strengths of TOC as follows: "It takes much of the guesswork out of business decisions. It can give a new person the tools to make decisions as good as someone with twenty years of experience."

Company J

Company J is a privately held company that manufactures custom metal-cutting tools and precision metal plugs and does some contract welding. Nearly all of the work is made to order. Ordinarily there is no excess capacity, and there has been only one layoff of employees in more than 60 years.

The custom metal-cutting tool industry is mature and is in decline due to a trend toward plastics and away from metals in fabrication—particularly in the automotive industry. Moreover, competitors from overseas have been entering the domestic market. The result of these trends is industry-wide excess capacity. No single company dominates the industry, but Company J is number one in its geographic area. All production is made to order, and the lead time is at present only three to five days.

Precision metal plugs are complex, highly machined parts used in specialized industrial applications. Precision plugs have much tighter tolerances than cutting tools. Company J jumped into this market about 10 years ago when it became clear that the cutting-tool market was in decline. One competitor dominates the precision plug market with 70% of the market. Company J focuses its efforts on "specials" rather than on the more standardized products. Most production is made to order, although the company maintains very small inventories of some standard plugs. The lead time for precision plugs at present is five to 10 days.

The company also does some contract welding—particularly of cut bar stock. Weldments, unlike precision plugs and cutting tools, are labor-intensive, low-tech products. This is a huge market, of which Company J has a very tiny portion, and weldments are a small part of the company's total sales.

Exhibit 3-2 contains a simplified flowchart of typical job routings in the shop. In general, Company J prefers to compete on quality and service rather than on price. The company has shorter lead times than its competitors and is on the cutting edge of technology. For example, the company is the first in its industry to accept digitized CAD drawings via modem from customers.

The former president of the company became interested in TOC after reading *The Goal,* and he passed the book around to managers in about 1988. Since that time five people have taken the Jonah course. The current top two managers were the first to take the course and their exposure to the Thinking Process in that course was very limited. The last two employees to have taken the course had extensive exposure to the Thinking Process. Jonah training was described by several people in the company as a humbling experience. "We found out that what we had been doing was wrong. We also learned to

Exhibit 3-2
Production Flowchart at Company J

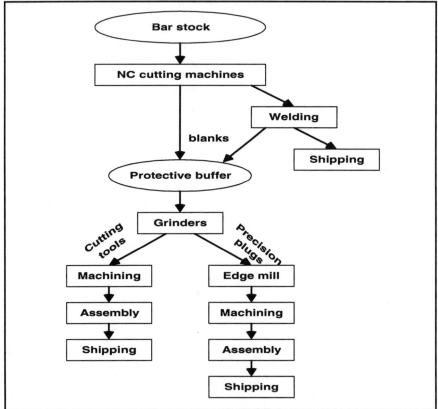

look inside our own area of responsibility to find problems and solutions. We learned not to point fingers." When asked about the importance of TOC to his company, the president said, "TOC is it." TOC is used to run the shop floor, to price products, and to guide strategy.

Management admits, with some humor, that their initial exposure to TOC was just enough to be dangerous. Armed with Throughput Accounting data that indicated fat margins, prices were cut 20%

across the board on a number of standard products. This tactic worked great for about a month until competitors reacted and dropped their prices, too. Prices did not recover after this skirmish and throughput declined. Management admits, "The first swing was a strike."

The focus shifted to the shop floor. Inventory was piled up in front of the grinders, which are used to grind and polish blanks prior to machining, and there was talk of buying a new grinder to relieve the congestion. However, TOC suggested that such situations are often the result of inappropriate policies rather than any real constraint. Upon closer inspection, it was discovered that blanks were being processed on the grinders in multiples of 10 in the interests of "processing efficiency." Because of this policy, blanks were being held up waiting for a batch of 10 to be processed. And if two blanks were urgently needed, 10 were run and the eight not really needed went into stock. Instead of buying a new machine, the rule was changed so that blanks were ground only as needed and in batch sizes of one if necessary. As a result of adopting this simple rule, cycle time in grinding dropped from six weeks to five days, and due date performance improved dramatically, throughput increased, work-in-process inventories decreased, and excess capacity on the numerical control (NC) cutting machines in front of the grinders was uncovered. With this simple change in the operating rules, there was enough capacity on the grinders to meet demand, and plans to purchase another machine were shelved.

Prior to TOC, a key performance measure was the ratio of indirect to direct hours, where direct hours consisted of all of the labor time written up on job tickets and indirect hours consisted of the remainder of the paid labor time except for enforced idleness due to machine breakdowns. Management admits that "every supervisor was pummeled on the indirect/direct ratio every week." Supervisors responded to this pressure by building to stock and by overreporting hours charged to jobs and overreporting hours lost due to machine breakdowns. It was a big cultural change to accept that some workers ought to be idle some of the time. Managers used to "stampede people out of the coffee lounge." Now it is understood that some idleness is okay, although idle time often is used for cross-training. (Labor classifications have dropped from 72 to six.)

Prior to TOC, operating expenses were controlled using flexible budgets that assumed costs are proportional to volume. Unfortunately, this view permitted operating expenses to drift up in good times. Now the flexible budgeting system is more sophisticated and resembles examples found in management accounting textbooks. Variances are computed by flexing only the totally variable costs and by treating operating expenses as fixed. For example, in the selling and administrative area, commissions, distributor discounts, delivery expense, and freight out are considered totally variable costs. If sales are up by 10%, the budget allowances for these items are increased by 10%. Everything else in selling and administration—including salaries, advertising and promotion, depreciation, telephone, office supplies, etc.—is considered fixed and actual costs are compared to budgeted costs without any adjustment for changes in volume. With the increase in volume the company has been experiencing, this system has put a brake on the growth in the fixed operating expenses.

Management has decided to operate "as if" the constraint is the grinders. These machines are toward the middle of the production process, which is a good place (for statistical reasons) to have buffer inventories. (Buffer inventories are required to protect the constraint.) And in fact these machines usually are the constraint. The grinders can be managed by moving jobs between the machines (they have slightly different capabilities) and by using a partial third shift. Bottlenecks sometimes temporarily crop up at other points, but these bottlenecks are almost always the result of poor policies. Change the policy and the bottleneck evaporates. Occasionally, capacity is added outside of the grinder area to eliminate an interactive constraint problem. For example, at one point the edge mills were identified as an interactive constraint. A somewhat dated used piece of equipment that could do edge mill work was purchased for $5,000. The payback on this investment was less than a month.

The management information system keeps track of the projected load, by day, on each of the grinder types. (See Exhibit 3-3 for an example of the constraint load report.) The company has a number

Exhibit 3-3
Company J Constraint Load Report

GRINDING CONSTRAINT LOAD					
LOAD FOR 06/21/93 THRU 07/02/93					
REPORT DATE 06/21/93					
Machine type	30mm	36mm	42mm	46mm	50mm
Daily capacity*	(600)	(1200)	(640)	(600)	(320)
	SCHEDULED USE				
06/21/93	(600)	(1340)	(430)	(220)	(50)
	100%	112%	67%	37%	16%
06/22/93	(870)	(890)	(540)	(310)	(310)
	145%	74%	84%	52%	97%
06/23/93	(980)	(400)	(130)	(390)	(70)
	163%	33%	20%	65%	22%
06/24/93	(240)	(140)	(70)	(0)	(50)
	40%	12%	11%	0%	16%
06/25/93	(180)	(60)	(240)	(0)	(0)
	30%	5%	38%	0%	0%

* Daily capacity is based on two shifts with 24 workers on each shift. In addition, a third shift with three workers can be used to take care of a backlog on any machine.

of different types of grinders largely distinguished by the size of blank that the machine can accommodate. The report provides the daily capacity on each type of machine for a two shift operation. The report also lists the requirements for each type of machine if the due dates on current orders are to be met. If the requirements exceed capacity, there are at least two remedies. First, if there is unused capacity on a machine with a larger size rating, work can be shifted up to that machine. For example, on 6/22/93 requirements exceed capacity on the 30mm machines by 45%. Some of this work can be shifted up to the 36mm machines. In addition, a partially manned third shift can be used to work off any backlogs that develop during the normal two-shift operation. The management information system also monitors requirements on nonconstraint resources to provide advance warnings of temporary bottlenecks that might appear on those resources. Management monitors the hours actually charged jobs as a percentage of hours available on the constraint to keep track of how well the constraint is being used. Underutilization of the constraint (as opposed to underutilization of nonconstraint resources) is considered a matter for management concern.

The marketing department in this company is responsible for drumming up requests for price quotes; marketing does not, however, set prices. That function is performed by the customer service department, which also negotiates due dates. Because lead time depends critically on the current loading on the constraint, customer service monitors the constraint load report closely. Manufacturing also provides customer service with guidelines to make sure the constraints are not overscheduled.

The management information system keeps track of throughput per constraint hour by job and in total on a daily basis in the "Contribution Report." (See Exhibit 3-4 for an example of such a report.) This data is important for monitoring the profitability of jobs and for estimating opportunity costs—particularly for pricing purposes. As previously mentioned, the company initially had cut prices substan-

Exhibit 3-4
Company J Contribution Report

Order Contribution Report for 06/21/93 through 06/21/93
Report date 06/21/93

Order Number	Gross Sales	Variable Costs	Thruput	Constraint Hours	Thruput per Hour
Cutting tools					
41631	796	394	402	N/A	N/A
41910	156	40	116	.51	227
42424	306	41	265	1.50	177
42659	262	79	183	.66	278
42692	288	61	227	.34	668
43227	422	63	359	.50	718

tially on certain standard products. At first they were swamped with orders. However, competitors eventually lowered their prices, and everyone in the industry wound up worse off than before. The company does not tinker with prices on standard products anymore—they basically are set in a competitive market. Pricing discretion is reserved for "specials." The pricing decision is of crucial importance in this market because in some product lines the company lands only about a quarter of the jobs it bids on—a circumstance the company is happy to live with if it gets the right jobs. Prices determine not only the revenue from the jobs the company gets but its product mix as well. The customer service manager, who is a recent Jonah, has designed an innovative computer-based system for supporting pricing decisions. With the aid of this support software, customer service uses price and due date promises to cherry pick the jobs the company really wants. Previously, prices were based on laborious full cost calculations, and it took two to three hours to assemble all of the required data and to carry out the computations. Now all of the data required to support the pricing decision are generated in 10 minutes.

The pricing system works as follows: Based on a few key characteristics of the job, a rough estimate is made of what the full cost price quote would have been under the old pricing system. Because it is only a rough estimate, it can be generated quickly. *The sole purpose of the full cost calculation is to arrive at an estimate of what the company's competitors will be quoting on the same job.*[2] The program then computes the throughput for the job, based on the assumption that the market price will be the full cost. To arrive at the throughput figure, materials costs, freight costs, and commissions are deducted from the assumed selling price. The throughput then is divided by the estimated amount of constraint time the job would require. The result is the throughput per constraint hour for the job. This figure is compared to the "target throughput per constraint hour," which is the minimum throughput per constraint hour the company would like to earn on all jobs. This target is set with reference to current opportunity costs. If the throughput per constraint hour is "awesome," the price may be shaved to ensure landing the job. If the throughput per constraint hour is too low, the price will be increased. If the company really doesn't want the job, the promised due date will be stretched out until it becomes uncomfortable for the customer. About 25% of capacity is reserved for "awesome" throughput per constraint hour jobs, with the remainder of the capacity going to lower throughput per constraint hour jobs. Over time the dividing line between "awesome" and other jobs, in terms of the required throughput per constraint hour, is adjusted to take up excess capacity. Management believes this pricing policy has been quite successful over the last two years.[3]

The pricing software also attacks the problem from a slightly different direction. A target price is computed based on materials costs, freight costs, commissions, the target throughput per constraint hour, and the amount of the constraint required for the job, as shown below.

Materials costs
+ Freight costs
+ Commissions
+ (Target throughput per constraint hour
   $\underline{\text{x constraint hours required})}$
$\underline{= \text{Target price}}$

This target price sets a floor on the price that can be quoted although circumstances may require that the floor be ignored for some customers or jobs.

In line with the pricing strategy, the company is considering changing its method of evaluating salespersons. Currently, they are evaluated on the number of orders they generate. Because the company would like to be able to cherry pick from among a large number of possible orders, it has been suggested that the salespersons be evaluated on the basis of the number of requests for price quotes they generate. The difference in performance measures is subtle but potentially very important.

At the time of our visit, management was wrestling with the problem of effectively segmenting the company's markets. The basic idea can be illustrated with a simple diagram (see Exhibit 3-5). In

Exhibit 3-5
Segmenting the Market

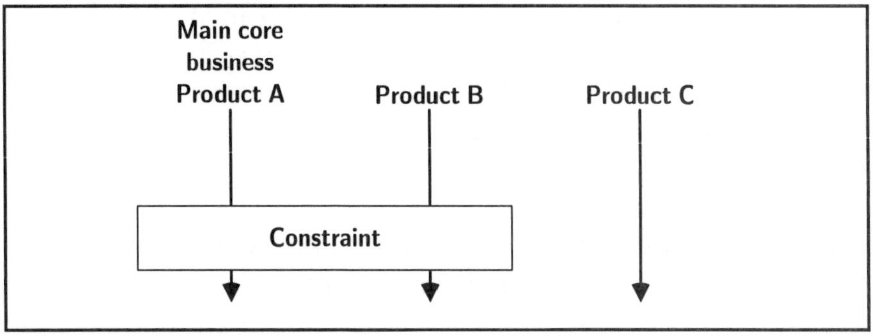

Company J, weldments are in the product C category. They do not require the use of the constrained resource, so obtaining more of this business does not incur any opportunity costs—at least up to the point where weldments create their own bottleneck. The identification of, and strategy with respect to, a product of type B is more critical. These products require the use of the constraint, but they are not part of the core business of the company. Ideally, the demand for product B should be negatively correlated with the demand for product A so that product B can take up any slack that is created as the result of fluctuations in the demand for product A. If demands for the two products are not naturally countercyclical, then ideally the company should be able to get into and out of the market for product B quickly without disrupting its market for product A or its future market for product B. This scenario suggests that: (1) the company should be a very small player in the market for product B so that fluctuations in its participation in the market would be largely unnoticed and that (2) the customer base for product B should be different from the company's core customer base.

To some degree, these conditions are met with the company's two main products—cutting tools and precision plugs. Cutting tools can be interpreted as the company's main core business. The company has as much as 30% of this market in its region, so it inevitably feels the results of fluctuations in the market. On the other hand, the company is a very small player in the precision plug market and can cherry pick its business. The difficulty the company faces at present is that when demand for cutting tools falls, the slack cannot be fully taken up with more precision plug work because any substantial expansion would be constrained by the capacity of the NC milling machines.

Jobs are scheduled using a DBR approach. The grinders are the drum and due dates are promised based on availability of time on the grinders. When an order is accepted, the job is first scheduled for a grinder and then, based on the lead time through the constraint (the rope), materials are scheduled for release to the job floor. Job tickets contain the release date, the date the job is scheduled for the constraint, and the due date.

When a DBR scheduling system was first used in 1990-1991, it was a "dream world." Throughput increased, work-in-process inventories decreased, due date performance was "unbelievable," lead times were 40% better than the competition's. The results exceeded everyone's expectations. The dream world ended after about three months. Management believes they were paying too much attention to keeping the DBR system working smoothly and meeting due dates and didn't notice a market downturn in time. Jobs were being released on schedule and due dates were being met, so they thought things were just fine. However, the constraint was being starved due to insufficient orders.

Now management closely monitors the protective buffers, which are supposed to be about half a day's work on the grinders. If the protective buffer is too large, there may be a problem such as downtime on the constraint. By looking at the job tickets management can determine quickly if jobs are past due for the grinders. If the protective buffer is too small, there is also likely a problem. For example, the buffer may shrink due to insufficient demand. At any rate, changes in the size of the protective buffer provide an important clue that something may be amiss.

Throughput Accounting is used internally, but some of the board of directors (the majority of whom are outside nonowners) still want to see GAAP financial reports, so the company keeps two sets of books. Financial statements based on both sets of books are presented to the board. The difference in net income between the two books is the change in labor and overhead capitalized in inventory using GAAP, so the only adjustment necessary is to inventories and cost of goods sold. Unfortunately, trends in net income between GAAP and Throughput Accounting books are often at odds. In the month prior to our visit, one of grinders broke down, which hurt throughput without any compensating decrease in operating expenses. However, work-in-process inventories piled up in front of the constraint, so net income was higher on a GAAP basis than on a Throughput Accounting basis.

The monthly internal Throughput Accounting reports include data on throughput, operating expenses, inventories, income before taxes (T-OE), return on investment ([T-OE]/assets), inventory turns (T/I), productivity (T/OE), throughput per employee (T/headcount), and throughput per constraint hour.

The formal Thinking Process is not used extensively at Company J although the customer service manager, one of the more recently trained Jonahs, frequently uses trees to analyze problems. Interestingly, he says that all of the constraints in his department are policy constraints—which trees are most effective in identifying and correcting.

The only attempt at the company to use trees in a group situation with non-Jonahs was a dud. There was too much finger-pointing. Everyone thought the core problem was someone else's problem. With non-Jonahs, management now uses "verbal trees" and is careful not to say who should be the one to take action—therefore avoiding assessing blame. Despite this circumspection, the correct actions generally are taken by the appropriate people.

The president summed up his company's experience with TOC as follows: "There is no way TOC is a passing fad. The 'hot books of the moment' each address a common bottleneck at a particular point in time. They solve problems, but the problems move. TOC is it for this company."

Western Textile Products

Western Textile Products is a privately held company in the textiles converting industry. Several aspects of this company's involvement in TOC were unusual. First, an unusually high proportion of management and supervisory personnel had completed Jonah training. At the time of our visit there were 36 Jonahs in the company, 19 of whom had been trained in an in-house Jonah course. Second, the company has two persons whose major responsibility is TOC training and facilitation. Probably as a consequence, the formal Thinking Process was used more extensively at this company than at just about any other site we visited. Despite a somewhat difficult period for the industry and increased competition, the company has experienced increased profits and return on investment and markedly reduced levels of work-in-process inventories. As one manager put it, "We have looked for bottlenecks all our lives, but did not realize their importance. We were putting out fires all the time. Now we can identify the constraint before it bites us in the butt." Another manager said, "Now when we fix something, it stays fixed."

The company is primarily a subcontractor for the apparel industry, supplying garment components such as pockets, waistbands, and cut fabric. The company's customers can (and sometimes do) make such components themselves, but Western Textile Products is generally more efficient and can pass on economies realized from purchasing raw materials on a large scale.

This industry is highly competitive, and it is important to be responsive to customers. Turnaround time is very short—three to seven days for most products. In recent years, the company's customers have been moving to JIT deliveries, which results in fluctuating demand and scheduling problems for the company. One manager stated, "Competition has been very intense for the last six to seven years. If we slip, we'll lose something big."

We visited three sites: corporate headquarters in St. Louis and manufacturing facilities in Greenville, South Carolina, and Columbus, Mississippi. Both of the plants are job shops in which nearly everything is made to order. The Greenville plant does contract textile cutting and slitting and makes sweatbands for baseball caps and waistbands and bindings for trousers. The Columbus plant does contract textile cutting and makes waistbands for work pants, pockets, and auto visor backing. Exhibit 3-6 shows a rough flowchart of a process found at both plants.

This is a mature, labor-intensive, low-tech industry. None of the equipment costs more than $250,000 and some equipment predates World War II. Having said that, many of the machines have been built or substantially modified by in-house mechanics, and this home-grown technology may be a source of some competitive advantage.

The company avoids layoffs; there has been only one layoff in the last 10 years, which was due to a factory closing. The company pays hourly wages at above-market rates, and everyone can work a steady 40-hour or more work week. If business slows down, occasionally someone volunteers to take time off, but no one *has* to go home. Consequently, with the exception of overtime, wages and salaries are essentially fixed and very predictable. The assumption commonly made in TOC that labor is fixed is reasonably valid in this particular company.

Prior to becoming involved in TOC, the company had a traditional labor productivity reporting system. Greg Holcombe, the production manager of the Greenville plant, says that it was just like in *The Goal*—the old production reports made people build excess work-in-process inventories. One manager admits that in one of the plants some of the bottleneck machines were being held in reserve to make sure that in case of a machine breakdown the operators would be busy all of the time. Perry Robbins, a Jonah and the production manager at the Columbus plant, says that in contrast to the old approach of keeping people as busy as possible, "the way to make money is to squeeze machines, not people."

Ann Prather, the production supervisor at Greenville and a Jonah, reports that "the operators were ecstatic when the old labor reporting system was abandoned. The paperwork was a constant irritant." At the Columbus plant it used to take about 20 minutes per day per worker to record the data required by the labor productivity report-

Exhibit 3-6
Textile Converting Flowchart
Western Textile Products

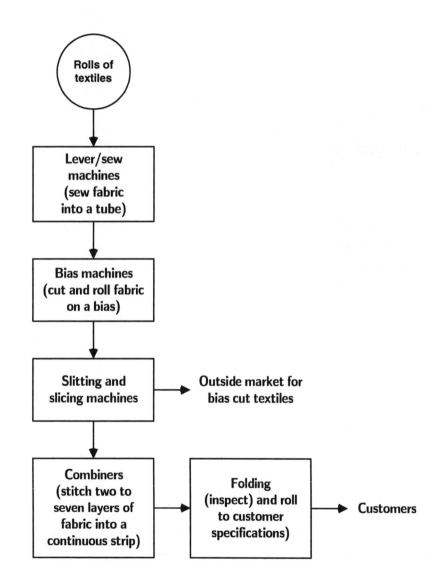

ing system, and it took a secretary half a day per week to compile the data to send to corporate headquarters.

Greg Holcombe, the production manager at Greenville and a Jonah, says that there have been some problems with idle workers in the new TOC environment. Some workers are uncomfortable being idle, and one worker even threatened to quit when the labor productivity reporting was abandoned because she could no longer brag about her high rate of output. Moreover, idle workers do create resentment among those who are not idle, and if you give idle workers brooms, they don't like it. Some workers will slow down their pace to keep from being tagged as idle. Unfortunately, once they have become accustomed to the slower pace it is difficult to pick up the pace later when really necessary.

To counteract these problems, there has been extensive cross-training of workers so that workers can be shifted from areas where there is little work to be done. However, application of TOC principles has uncovered so much excess capacity at Greenville that the ultimate solution is going to be to transfer some workers to a new facility being built nearby.

TOC has led to a focus on improving the bottleneck operations. It generally is agreed in the company that just about any production bottleneck can be broken by changing policies or modifying processes at very little cost. At the Greenville plant, the slitting machines, which are used to slit large rolls of textiles, appeared to be a constraint. The plant was doing a lot of contract slitting, so two more machines were purchased and management was contemplating adding a second shift. However, before the additional workers were hired, some tests were run. The tests revealed that the slitting machines were being run on average only one hour in a nine-hour shift. The other eight hours were required to get materials, load and unload the machine, and do setups. Instead of adding a second shift, a second person was assigned to each machine to fetch materials and do as much of the setting up as possible off-line while the machine was running. This solution increased the run time per shift to four hours from the previous one hour. Had another shift been added and the old procedures followed, the cost would have been higher and the run time would have increased by only one hour.

At one point the "baloney slicers," which cut roll goods, appeared to be a constraint. About 500 rolls of material that had been processed through the bias machines (which are themselves a constraint) were waiting to be cut on these machines. Greenville has four baloney slicers—two manual and two automatic. The manual machines actually have a higher rate of output than the automatic machines, but they were idle 60% of the time because workers were busy setting up and monitoring the automatic machines. The solution was to shut off the automatic machines—something that would never have been done before TOC due to the negative impact on the utilization rates for the automatic machines. The output of the work center went up by 40%, and the work-in-process inventories were largely eliminated.

At Greenville, the bias machines are the real constraint when the constraint is not in the market. There are two of these machines, which cut and roll fabric on a bias prior to other operations. This constraint has been elevated in several ways. First, additional workers have been cross-trained to operate the machines, and they are used on an overtime basis as needed. Second, setups have been streamlined. Cutting bars on the machine contain cutting tools spaced at specific intervals for each product. Each time there was a changeover, the machine was shut down, the cutting bar was removed, and cutting tools were attached. Then the whole assembly was put back in position. The bulk of the time in this setup is the attachment of the cutting tools. To reduce the idle time during setups, two more cutting bars were fabricated. The cutting tools now are attached to the cutting bars off-line while the machine is running, and then the cutting bars are rotated with each new product. Finally, at the time of our visit a new bias machine was being built in-house.

Because the bias machines are the constraint, they serve as the drum in the DBR scheduling system at Greenville. The protective buffer in front of the bias machines represents only about one to two hours of work. Ann Prather, the production supervisor at Greenville, states that it took only about a day and a half to design the DBR scheduling rules for the plant. The results were immediate—the backlog of 700,000 yards was cut in half within one month.

At Columbus several independent production processes are used for different products. The plant's major product is waistbands. The constraint on the waistband line is the combining machines, basically sewing machines that automatically stitch together up to seven different layers of fabric. The combiners are fed from rolls of fabric typically only a few inches wide. If two layers of fabric are stitched together, then the machine is fed from two rolls. If three layers are stitched, the machine is fed from three rolls, and so on. Several actions have been taken to make processing on the constraint more efficient (that is, elevate the constraint). Larger rolls of the input fabric are prepared (a longer strip of fabric is wound onto each roll). This increase in size reduces the number of changeovers required because rolls of fabric are exhausted less frequently. In addition, the number of machines being run by each operator is being reduced, which increases labor requirements but is more than offset by the increased throughput.

Back pockets are made at Columbus using an entirely different process. When this process was first examined using TOC principles, hot slitting was the constraint. Efforts then were concentrated on discovering how to increase the hot slitting throughput rate. Textiles were being processed as if they were all the same, but investigation revealed that some textiles could be processed faster than others. Moreover, by controlling the heat of the knives, defects could be reduced and the processing speed increased. Matching the processing rate to the textile and controlling the heat of the knives doubled the average rate of output. The constraint on the back pocket line then shifted to edge creasers. An edge creaser is a fairly simple piece of equipment, so another one was built in-house. Then the constraint shifted to the rotary cutter—another fairly simple piece of equipment. Once again management responded by building more equipment in-house. At that point the constraint shifted to the market, that is, the capacity of the process exceeded market demand. The general feeling at Western Textile Products is that by changing policies, tweaking the process, and perhaps spending a few dollars, the constraint almost always will shift to the market.

At Columbus temporary bottlenecks crop up unexpectedly due to changes in product mix. They usually are dealt with by shifting workers from nonbottleneck work centers to the temporary bottleneck. This strategy may seem obvious, but in a conventional manufacturing facility it may not be so evident which work centers are really bottlenecks because all work centers are kept busy all of the time—producing to stock if necessary. In a TOC environment producing to stock to keep busy is prohibited, and it is much clearer which work centers have excess capacity and can therefore lose some of it on a temporary basis.

Recently, cash was a constraint, so the focus at corporate headquarters was on throughput per dollar of working capital (T/WC). Actions taken included implicitly dropping some customers and products with low T/WC ratios by raising prices. Unfortunately, management admits that inertia took over and people were still focusing on this particular measure even after the cash crunch passed.

TOC has changed the company's pricing strategy. David Thraikill, the vice president in charge of operations at Greenville and a Jonah, says that before TOC people got nervous if the market price fell below a product's standard cost. It now is understood that anything above materials cost is okay if there is idle capacity. And, when there is no excess capacity, orders should be evaluated by comparing incremental throughput with incremental operating expenses. (When the plant is "at capacity," overtime is used to handle additional work.) As a consequence, the company is accepting orders at prices it would have passed up before. Also, it is understood that even though the constrained resource may be at capacity, work that doesn't require the use of that resource can still be picked up at seemingly low prices. On the other hand, Thraikill cautioned that you should be careful about cutting prices on core business. If you do cut prices for established customers because of competitive conditions and idle capacity, you should tell them why you are doing it and explain it may be a temporary phenomenon.

At corporate headquarters, the company's pricing policy was explained as follows. In the past the company attempted to set prices to maintain gross margins on fully allocated costs. Because of competitive conditions, some product lines were dropped because of "inadequate" gross margins. It now is acknowledged that this policy was a mistake and, if left unchecked, could have led to a death spiral. Now the company accepts whatever prices are dictated by market conditions. On new products, a target price is set by marking up only materials costs. The markup is based on the usual markup on materials costs in the market rather than on any calculations aimed toward "recovering" unallocated costs.

Throughput Accounting has been adopted and charts are maintained on a 12-month rolling average basis for throughput, operating expenses, inventories, profit, and return on assets. Only minor adjustments are required to convert these statements to GAAP financial reports because the company holds very small inventories.

Corporate headquarters has created a valuing worksheet for summarizing the financial impacts of major decisions (see Exhibit 3-7). The worksheet requires the preparer to estimate the impact of an action on sales, materials costs, throughput, operating expenses, profit, inventory, accounts receivable, accounts payable, working capital, fixed assets, return on assets, number of employees, and profit per employee. This worksheet focuses on changes so it is entirely consistent with the familiar relevant cost approach to decision making.

Exhibit 3-7
The Valuing Worksheet
Western Textile Products

SITUATION: _____ DATE: _____
OPTION: _____ BY: _____

LOCATION: _____ LEVEL: [ ] Corporation [ ]
Division

		CURRENT	+ CHANGE	= FUTURE

	Sales (K$/Y)		☐	
-	Material (K$/Y)		☐	
=	Throughput	☐	☐	☐
- Operating Expense (K$/Y)		☐	☐	☐
=	Profit (K$/Y)	☐	☐	☐

	Inventory (K$)		☐	
+	Accounts Receivable (K$)		☐	
-	Accounts Payable (K$)		☐	
=	Working Capital (K$)		☐	
+	Fixed Assets (K$)		☐	
=	Assets (K$)	☐	☐	☐

	Profit (K$/Y)			
÷	Assets (K$)			
=	ROA	☐		☐

	Profit (K$/Y)			
÷	# Employees	☐	☐	☐
=	ROE	☐		☐

NOTES OR ASSUMPTIONS:

_____
_____

Exhibit 3-8
The Credit Hold Current Reality Tree
Western Textile Products

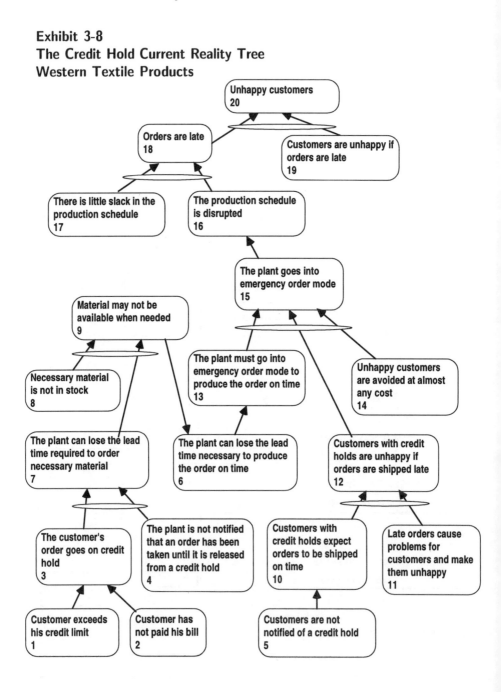

Ironically, there is more frustration and dissatisfaction with the level of involvement in the Thinking Process at this company than in any other company we visited. And yet the formal Thinking Process is used more often and by more people here than anywhere else, with the exception of Kent Moore Cabinets. Trees are used to address all kinds of problems at all levels of the company. Indeed, the president, Charlie Van Dyke, would like to see a formal TP analysis of any major decision that comes across his desk. For example, at the time of our visit trees were being used to develop the annual business plan. There also was ample evidence that trees are used frequently by some people at the local level, although often with the help of one of the TOC facilitators from corporate headquarters.

An edited example of a Current Reality Tree prepared at the Greenville plant is displayed in Exhibit 3-8. This tree is fairly simple with only one Undesirable Effect—namely, customers unhappy with late shipments. (The tree is being used here precisely because it is simple. We were shown far more complex trees during our visit.) The fact that the tree is labelled the "Credit Hold" Current Reality Tree indicates that the preparer of the tree probably knew that credit holds were contributing to the problem even before starting the tree. In analyses that involve multiple UDEs, the core problems are usually not so transparent before the analysis is begun. Even so, this CRT provides a compact way to communicate the preparer's analysis of the problem to others. We will spend some time going over this tree because it illustrates several important points.

The numbers in the boxes have no significance; they are simply a way to identify a box quickly. Starting at the bottom of the tree, both box 1 and box 2 have arrows that lead into box 3. The connections should be read as follows: If the customer exceeds his or her credit limit *or* the customer has not paid the bill, then the order goes on hold. To use more technical language, the existence of the entity in box 1 is sufficient but not necessary for the existence of the entity in box 3. The customer's exceeding the credit limit is sufficient to cause a credit hold, but it is not the only way because a credit hold also can happen through the additional cause of a customer not paying the bill. Likewise, the existence of the entity in box 2 is sufficient but not necessary for the existence of the entity in box 3.

Moving upward in the tree, we see that boxes 3 and 4 have arrows pointing to box 7 and that these arrows are connected by an elliptical "banana." The banana modifies the meaning of the arrows. The arrows now should be read as follows: If the order goes on credit hold *and* the plant is not notified that an order has been taken until it is released from credit hold, the plant can lose the lead time required to order necessary material. In this case, the existence of the entities in boxes 3 and 4 are jointly sufficient to produce the entity in box 7; that is, both acting together can cause the result. However, both are required to cause the result. If either of the entities in boxes 3 and 4 does not exist, then the entity in box 7 may not exist either. The importance of this fact is that it may be possible to break the causal chain by eliminating just one of the conditions. In this case, it may be possible to set up a system in which the plant is notified that an order has been taken when the order is put on credit hold.

Continuing upward in the CRT in rapid succession, the links between boxes 3, 4, and 7 should be read: If an order goes on credit hold *and* the plant is not notified that an order has been taken until the order is released from credit hold, then the plant can lose the lead time necessary to order material. The links between boxes 7, 8, and 9 should be read: If the plant can lose the lead time required to order necessary material *and* the necessary material is not in stock, then the material may not be available when needed. And if the material is not available when needed (box 9), then the plant can lose the lead time necessary to produce the order (box 6). If the plant loses the lead time necessary to produce the order (box 6) then the plant must go into emergency order mode to produce the order on time (box 13). Moving back toward the bottom of the tree, if customers are not notified of credit holds (box 5), then customers with credit holds expect their orders to be shipped on time (box 10). If customers with credit holds expect their orders to be shipped on time (box 10) *and* late orders cause customers problems (box 11), then customers with credit holds are unhappy if orders are shipped late (box 12). If the plant must go into an emergency order mode to produce the order on time (box 13) *and* customers with credit holds are unhappy if orders are shipped late (box 12) *and* unhappy customers are avoided at almost any cost (box 14), then the plant goes into emergency order mode (box 15). If the plant goes into emergency order mode (box 15), then the production schedule is disrupted (box 16). If the production schedule is disrupted (box 16) *and* there is little slack in the production schedule (box 17), then orders with and without prior credit holds are late (box 18). If orders are late (box 18) *and* customers are unhappy if orders are late (box 19), then there are unhappy customers (box 20).

Apart from the insight developed by building such a tree, the tree immediately provides clues as to what actions might be taken to eliminate the Undesirable Effects (UDEs). In this case, the ultimate UDE is unhappy customers (box 20), although going into emergency order mode (box 15) and disruption of the production schedule (box 16) also may be considered UDEs. The key to eliminating UDEs is to examine the conditions that the preparer can control, which, if eliminated, would result in the removal of all of the UDEs.

In this case the most likely candidates for action are box 4, the plant is not notified that an order has been taken until released from credit hold, and box 5, the customer is not notified of a credit hold on his or her order. Eliminating either of these conditions would break the entire chain as constructed. This is not to say, however, that the solution is simply to notify the plant that an order has been taken before it is released from credit hold or to notify the customer of a credit hold on the order. Matters are seldom that simple and that is the reason for proceeding through the subsequent steps of building the Evaporating Cloud, Prerequisite Tree, Transition Tree, and

Future Reality Tree. There may be negative implications that should be dealt with before taking a seemingly simple action such as notifying customers of credit holds.

Exhibit 3-9 is an edited version of Greenville's Future Reality Tree for dealing with the credit hold problem. Note that the proposed solution is more complex (and more comprehensive) than simply notifying the plant and customers about credit holds. This more complete solution was suggested initially by observing from the CRT that proper notifications to the plant and to customers should eliminate the problem with late shipments due to order holds.

We also were shown a fairly complete set of trees having to do with the acquisition of a major new facility at Greenville that would use sophisticated computerized equipment to do contract cutting. The trees were used to investigate the feasibility of the project, and once it had been approved by management, were used to present the project to the company's owners and bankers. We were told that the bankers had no difficulty following the presentation based on trees and the process of acquiring approval went exceptionally smoothly. The Transition Tree for the project now is being used to schedule the major steps in the project.

Regarding the importance of the Thinking Process (TP), Dan Lilienkamp, one of the two TOC facilitators at the company, says, "We have tried to focus on TP lately since our own policies are usually responsible for problems. We would have to do archeological research to find out why we have some of these policies." Unfortunately, as pointed out by the company president Charlie Van Dyke, "Some people adapt to TP very quickly; with others it is like pulling teeth."

Dan Lilienkamp agrees with this assessment and adds, "About a quarter of the Jonahs are comfortable with TP and can do it on their own. Another half of the Jonahs believe in the TP process but need help to do it. The remaining quarter of the Jonahs don't really believe in the usefulness of TP."

Exhibit 3-9
The Credit Hold Future Reality Tree—Western Textile Products

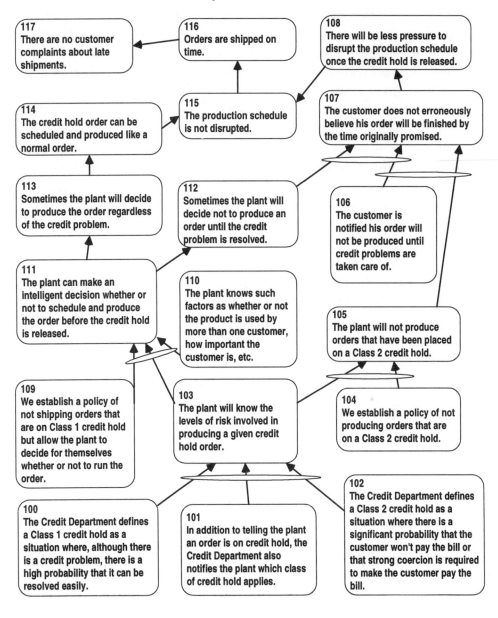

Some of the TP tools are understood and accepted more than others. People—even those not trained in TP—often understand and like Current Reality Trees. However, people have difficulty understanding Evaporating Clouds, and they tend to view Future Reality Trees with skepticism. There is little familiarity in the company with Prerequisite Trees and Transition Trees—probably because they are relatively new tools.

Nevertheless, the vast majority of the people we talked to in the company are convinced there is a big payoff to using the Thinking Process on substantial problems but that it requires practice, time, and discipline. One manager who uses trees only occasionally said, "Doing trees forces you to look at all of the positives and negatives. If you have a real solid tree, you have confidence. Another plus is that everyone involved in the process of building a tree eventually buys in."

Thrailkill, who is the vice president in charge of operations at Greenville and a Jonah, believes that when trees are used to analyze a problem and develop an action plan in a team setting, it is almost impossible not to get buy-in. The process of developing the trees should address any reasonable objections. He also believes that the Thinking Process has brought focus to meetings that in the past did not accomplish much. He cautions, however, that a manager must be willing to go with the results of the process and not dictate a solution.

Charlie Van Dyke summed up the company's experience with TOC as follows: "The organization has not been improving at the rate leading Jonahs would like to see. TOC is the right track, but there are still a lot of problems to tackle. For example, measurements don't always line up with what people should be doing." We caution the reader not to interpret this as an unduly negative assessment. As Shigeo Shingo points out: "It is a universal truth that those who are not dissatisfied will never make progress. . . . *[D]issatisfaction is the mother of improvement.*"[4]

Samsonite Europe N.V.

Samsonite Europe N.V., a subsidiary of Samsonite Inc., produces and sells "hard-side" and "soft-side" luggage in Europe. The company sells more than 550 different combinations of individual items and colors directly to about 8,000 customers, most of whom are retailers.

Production of soft-side luggage is labor intensive and there are many local competitors—many of whom subcontract manufacturing in the Far East. Production of hard-side luggage, on the other hand, is relatively capital intensive. Each item in a luggage line requires two custom-made injection molds (one for the top shell and one for the bottom shell), each of which costs hundreds of thousands of dollars. Consequently, there are relatively few competitors in this market.

Traditionally, luggage is made on an assembly line. Some parts are purchased and others (mainly shells and metal frames) are manufactured on site. Each operator on the assembly line carries out a few simple operations—for example, drilling holes in the shell. A simplified flowchart of a typical traditional assembly line is displayed in Exhibit 3-10. In such an assembly line each piece of completed luggage is inspected and, if defective, is reworked by a specialist. With the exception of rework, the individual operations are simple enough that training takes very little time and an individual can attain proficiency very quickly. However, quality control is difficult on such a line—marred finishes are a particular problem. Because each piece of luggage is handled many times and by many different people, damage can easily occur. When it does, it is difficult to trace down the source. Also, the pace of the assembly line is set by the pace of the slowest worker on the line. If one person has to take a break the whole line is shut down. Finally, statistical fluctuations cause the sorts of problems with floating bottlenecks, inventory buildups, and reduced throughput described in *The Goal*.

Samsonite Europe N.V. operates seven factories, each specializing in a few product lines. Some factories make hard-side luggage, some make soft-side luggage, and a few produce both product lines. All of the output of all of the factories is shipped to a central warehouse in Belgium, which fills customer orders. In the past, there has

Exhibit 3-10
Traditional Hard-side Luggage Assembly Line
Samsonite Europe N.V.

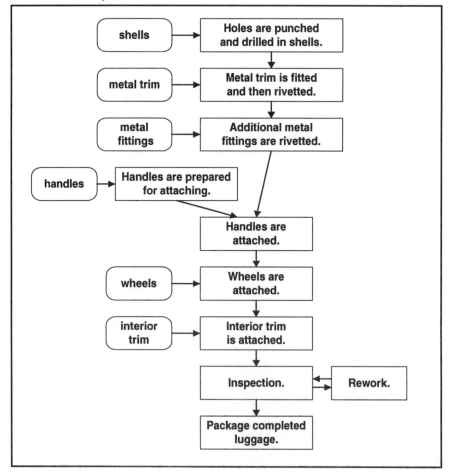

been a problem with a mismatch between what was on the shelf and what customers wanted. This problem was particularly serious because of the way in which out-of-stock items are handled. If an item ordered by a customer is not in stock, it is not backordered or entered into the manufacturing schedule. Instead, when the customer receives a shipment of in-stock items, out-of-stock items are flagged with the suggestion that the customer reorder the item later. This system has led to a number of undesirable effects including lost sales and precautionary overordering of the most popular products by some customers. While managers involved in manufacturing and sales would like to change this policy, it is unlikely to happen in the near future. In the past, up to 25% of items ordered have been out-of-stock at the time of order and were counted as "missed sales."

Missed sales were not due to an overall inadequate level of finished goods in the warehouse—on average, there were two months of finished goods inventory in the warehouse at any given time. There was, however, a mismatch between what was being manufactured and what was being sold. The result was missed sales and product obsolescence problems. The mismatch had a lot to do with how production was scheduled. Lead times were four to eight weeks on most products, so factory scheduling was frozen two months in advance based on sales forecasts made each month. In addition, factories were evaluated to a large extent on labor efficiency—the ratio of labor hours earned to labor hours paid. The labor hours earned during a period were determined by multiplying the period's output of each item by the standard direct labor hours allowed for the item. The drive for 100% (or better) labor efficiencies led to running all of the assembly lines as much as possible. And because each assembly line could handle only a limited range of product lines, there was a tendency to build excess inventories of finished goods for the less popular lines. Meanwhile, the production lines for the more popular lines also were running at their apparent capacities but were unable to satisfy demand.

In 1988 Wilfried Van Hove, the vice president of operations, began suggesting that employees in the company read *The Goal.* Marc Matton, then a manager in purchasing, read the book but felt that it had little relevance to purchasing. Shortly thereafter he was appointed managing director of the Henin Beaumont factory Samsonite in France, and he revived his interest in TOC. In 1990 both Van Hove and Matton attended the Jonah course. About 35 people also have attended a two-day workshop on TOC.

The Henin Beaumont factory that Matton was taking over had been built in 1984 and had a relatively young and adaptable workforce. Unfortunately, labor relations were poor, probably due to the rather autocratic approach of its outgoing managing director. While this auto cratic approach may have been useful in getting the new factory on its feet, it had apparently outlived its usefulness by 1989. Because of the delicate labor relations, Matton was particularly careful to involve the plant's workforce in his planning.

Matton believes that the Current Reality Tree he developed for Henin Beaumont was very important in understanding the situation at the plant. Despite his limited experience in manufacturing, TOC helped him to identify core problems and to come up with solutions that he was able to sell to others. Within a very short time Matton initiated radical changes. With the support of top management, much of the factory was gutted and the assembly process was reorganized. Instead of assembly lines in which a dozen or so workers each performed a single simple task, production cells were formed. (A simplified flowchart for a typical production cell appears in Exhibit 3-11.) A production cell consists of one or more preparation workers, a kit assembler, and a number of assemblers. A single person (sometimes aided by an idle assembler) gathers together all of the parts required to make a piece of luggage and places them inside the luggage shell. This "kit" is placed in a temporary buffer area. Up to 10 assembly workers pull kits from the buffer and each completely assembles the piece of luggage from the kit. When done, the worker sends the finished luggage on to packing and pulls another kit from the buffer. Each assembler is responsible for the quality of his or her own work; however, pieces of luggage are randomly selected for inspection by a quality auditor.

Exhibit 3-11
Hard-side Luggage Production Cell
Samsonite Europe N.V.

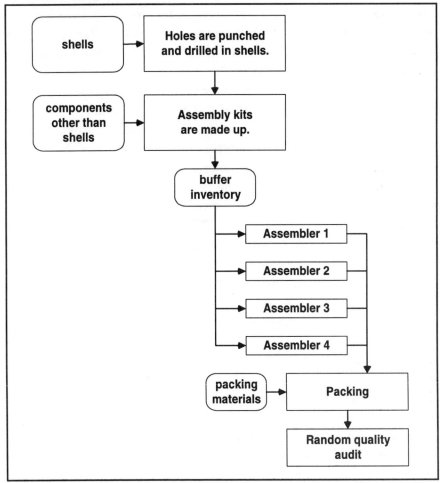

This system has a number of advantages over the old assembly line operation. Fewer people handle each item, and each item is moved around and picked up and put down much less frequently, reducing damage. In addition, the rate of output no longer is determined by the slowest worker on the line, and the whole line does not have to stop every time a worker has to take a break.

While most production was switched over to production cells, some traditional assembly lines were retained, particularly for older products. New employees are started on the assembly lines because the task is very simple and can be mastered quickly. Some workers prefer the assembly lines because they require little thinking and it is easier to converse on the job.

The reorganization did have its costs. Some new equipment was required and the plant layout had to be changed. Another cost was that workers had to be trained to do more tasks. To provide incentives, the base salary of a worker was increased if he or she became certified in additional tasks. Some products had to be redesigned so that they could be produced in the new production cells. In particular, rather than purchasing a big riveting machine for each assembler, products were redesigned so that they could be assembled with screws and an electric screwdriver. All of this increased operating expenses, but offsetting this increase was a reduction in indirect labor—quality inspectors and other forms of indirect labor were no longer so necessary. The improved operations created capacity that eventually was used to add another product line and to reduce the missed sales problem. The net effect was that within one year, gross margins increased by 100% with essentially no change in operating expenses.

These changes had the immediate effect of causing a temporary decline in labor efficiencies. While workers were being retrained and the plant was being reorganized, production fell, which decreased the numerator in the labor efficiency ratio. Moreover, when indirect workers were transferred into the production area, they were reclassified as direct labor, which increased the denominator in the labor efficiency ratio. For about six months, the labor efficiencies at the Henin Beaumont plant suffered and higher management voiced concern. However, patience was rewarded. Between 1989 and 1992, work-in-process inventories were down from about six weeks of sales to two weeks of sales. Lead time was cut from about six weeks to one week. Missed sales (as a percentage of units ordered) were down from about 25% to about 5%. Seconds (low-quality output) were down from about 2% to 1% of hard-side production and from 5% to 1% of soft-side production. Indirect labor (mostly inspection labor) had been virtually eliminated.

Due to reduced lead times, the planning cycle was down to one week, enabling a radical overhaul of the production scheduling system. Instead of scheduling based on two-month forecasts, the plant now could respond quickly to changes in market demands, almost as they occurred. In addition, multifunction training of workers permitted the scheduler to shift workers from one assembly area to another as the need arose. As a consequence, labor was now the constraint.

Scheduling now was based on the weekly throughput priority list, an edited copy of which appears as Exhibit 3-12. This list contains both a "to-do list" and a "not-to-do list." The to-do list shows all of the products that, based on recent sales history, will be out of stock within the next 10 days if there is no new production. The to-do list is prioritized in terms of the "estimated missed throughput" for each product. (A better ordering would be provided by dividing the estimated missed throughput by the direct labor hours required to produce that throughput because direct labor is the constraint.) By focusing on these units, management concentrates production resources on the products that will provide the largest potential throughput if current sales trends continue.

The not-to-do list shows the products that will continue to have excess stocks even if there is no additional production. This list is

Exhibit 3-12
Priority List*

3 December 1991
Short Horizon: 10 day
To-Do List

Product	Units in stock	Unit sales per day	Days c verage	Est. missed units	Throughput per unit (BF)	Est. missed Throughput (BF)
Synchro	3,646	503	7.2	1,384	1,413	1,955,592
Madeira	1,002	168	6.0	678	1,780	1,206,840
Sampan	275	47	5.9	195	2,405	468,975
Onyx	127	31	4.1	183	2,163	395,829
Sapphire	222	38	5.8	158	2,271	358,818
Jubilee	229	35	6.5	121	2,395	289,795
Turbo	274	39	7.0	116	2,413	279,908
Milos	275	38	7.2	105	2,333	244,965
Jumbo	45	7	6.4	25	3,789	94,725
Emerald Kit	186	46	4.0	274	256	70,144
Airbus	1	1	1.0	9	1,891	17,019

Not-To-Do List

Product	Units in stock	Unit sales per day	Days coverage	Est. excess units	Throughput per unit (BF)	Est. excess inv. $ days (BF)
Yacht	7,294	136	53.6	5,934	2,077	268,882,586
Buggy	7,911	174	45.5	6,171	2,348	256,938,948
Observer	2,704	29	93.2	2,414	2,449	246,056,772
Inspector	2,716	37	73.4	2,346	2,494	185,490,104
Day tripper	269	1	269.0	259	4,702	157,707,431
Economist	1,342	7	191.7	1,272	1,259	145,502,990
Oyster A	562	5	112.4	512	4,836	126,772,838
Tiffany	1,354	16	84.6	1,194	2,438	108,615,643
Jasmine	609	2	304.5	589	1,133	98,265,373
Prestige	417	3	139.0	387	3,053	76,207,460
Safari	134	1	134.0	124	2,384	18,328,192

Days coverage = Units in stock / Unit sales per day
Estimated missed units = Unit sales per day x Horizon —Units in stock
Throughput per unit (BF) is the selling price less materials costs per unit in Belgian francs
Estimated missed throughput (BF) = Estimated missed units x throughput per unit (BF)
Estimated excess units = Units in stock - Unit sales per day x horizon
Estimated excess inventory $ days (BF) = Throughput per unit (BF) x estimated excess units
x ((Days coverage – Horizon)/2)

* The data are disguised.

prioritized on the basis of "estimated excess inventory-dollar-days"—
a measure based on the "inventory-dollar-days" measure that appears in Goldratt's writings. If a unit with a selling price of $10 and
with a materials cost of $4 is held in inventory for five days, then its
inventory-dollar-days would be computed as $30—$6 of throughput for each of five days. The excess inventory-dollar-days is an
estimate of the total inventory-dollar-days that will be incurred until all existing stocks have been depleted. Van Hove commented
that the estimated excess inventory-dollar-days measure lacks credibility and meaning to many people because it is such a large number. He suggested that, instead, it might be better to convert it to a
measure of the holding cost by applying a fixed daily percentage
charge.

The to-do list is used to schedule what will be produced and how
it will be produced. Because workers are cross-trained, production
cells can be used to make a variety of different products and individual workers can be moved from idle production cells to active production cells. Before the Priority List was introduced, the percentage of missed sales in terms of throughput often exceeded the percentage of missed sales in terms of units ordered. That is no longer
the case and missed throughput ordinarily is insignificant, although
missed sales in terms of units ordered still average around 5%. On
the negative side, Van Hove and Matton say they initially underestimated how much buffer was needed in finished goods inventories to accommodate surges in demand, and as a result sales were
missed on an extremely popular new product.

Partly as a means to communicate with top management and
partly as a means of keeping score within the plant itself, Matton
developed a Henin Beaumont Plant Activity Dashboard, a two-page
monthly summary of the results of operations. This report contains
data on throughput, operating expenses, inventories, missed sales
due to out-of-stock situations, and TOC productivity measures.
Throughput in the report is defined as sales from the central ware-

house less materials costs at standard. That is, the factory does not receive credit on this report for its production until it is sold. (Note that this limitation was Matton's idea, rather than an idea imposed from above.) Because of it, there is a lag between the time when operating expenses appear on the report and when the resulting throughput appears on the report. Most accountants probably would object that recording operating expenses and throughput in this way violates the matching principle, although it is completely consistent with Goldratt's views of accounting. If this lag is measured in weeks, as is generally the case at Henin Beaumont, it is not a severe problem. However, longer lags would make it very difficult to evaluate a factory's current period performance fairly and might create difficulties in applying throughput accounting in other situations.

An interesting feature of the Activity Dashboard is that it includes summary data concerning labor efficiencies. In the past, attempts to improve labor efficiencies had led to operating problems, so one might wonder why labor efficiencies are still being reported. The reason is that due to the reorganization of the factory, labor is the constraint. As with any constraint, it is important to monitor its efficiency and utilization. Potential problems with using labor to produce to stock are much less likely now because controls on what is released to production are much tighter.

Samsonite Europe is involved in TQM, JIT, and statistical process control. No one perceived any conflicts between TOC and the other programs—at the company people saw significant synergies. Indeed, it was difficult for us to separate the influences of TOC from the influences of JIT, TQM, and other lean manufacturing techniques in the improvements that had been made. If any separation is possible, TOC provided the focus and grand strategy for change, and lean manufacturing (e.g., production cells) provided the specific means.

At the time of our visit Matton had just been promoted to director of sales of Samsonite Europe—his second lateral and vertical move in the organization in four years. He was planning his change strategies using formal trees. For example, he intended to switch the basis of salespersons' compensation from sales to throughput and was developing Prerequisite Trees and Transition Trees to plan the process of buy-in for this major step. Matton expressed confidence in the process and felt 90% sure he would get buy-in because of his thorough planning.

Company Q

Company Q is a small European company that makes handling equipment for the canning industry. This industry, like many others, has been undergoing substantial technological change. About 10 years ago, the Japanese began selling automated machines that ran at much higher speeds (up to 10 times as fast) and that demanded tighter tolerances. Because Company Q's products link such machines, their products had to be reengineered to work optimally with the new automated equipment.

This requirement posed a serious technical problem that ultimately was solved. The solution was expensive, however, and would appeal only to the top end of the market. After some soul-searching, Company Q decided to go for the best and to concentrate on this market niche. With this strategy they hoped to have enough orders (five to 10 per year) to keep everyone employed, to earn a good profit, and to maintain a good reputation.

The strategy was quite successful at first but, unfortunately, conditions changed. By the time the recession hit, the canning industry had installed too much capacity, and most customers had been acquired by much larger companies. Company Q found that it was much harder to sell these larger organizations on the advantages of higher-end equipment. The decision makers were too remote from operations to understand why it might be necessary to pay a substantial premium for a machine with a few more features. By late 1992 Company Q was in serious financial difficulty. Orders weren't coming in and customers were calling up to cancel existing orders.

Back in 1990, the managing director of the company, J. Gruen, had read *The Goal* and bought a number of copies that he handed out to employees. He was disappointed to discover that most employees weren't used to reading books and were having difficulty getting through *The Goal*. (Company Q is located in a country that generally is considered to have one of the highest literacy rates in the world.) Because he felt the message was important, he switched to a different format and held voluntary meetings in the evening at which he taught concepts from *The Goal* and *The Race*. Attendance at these meetings was high. Gruen believes that attitudes have changed partially as a result of these meetings; people now understand that the company is a system rather than just a collection of independent centers. Previously, if there was a problem the attitude was "the guys in the other department have a problem." Now the attitude is more likely to be "we have a problem."

Gruen took the first Jonah course in Europe in 1991 that worked with formal trees. This course generally was considered to be a failure by both the participants and the Avraham Goldratt Institute. Gruen believes that trees are a good way to understand a problem but are too complex and artificial to use on a daily basis. He feels that he just doesn't have the time to sit down and do trees. However, he does apply TOC philosophy on an informal basis—particularly effect-cause-effect thinking and Evaporating Clouds. Gruen provided us with several examples of the informal use of the Evaporating Cloud technique. These examples are discussed below.

Returning to the 1992 crisis, because there were no jobs on the order book it was obvious that operating expenses had to be reduced, and very quickly. Under local law, it is very difficult to lay off employees. At least one month's notice must be given and then there is a long administrative process that can drag on for months. The only way employees can be laid off immediately is by filing for bankruptcy. Filing for bankruptcy, however, would jeopardize the viability of the company and the jobs of those who remained. It would be possible to ask employees to leave voluntarily, but under the unemployment compensation laws, those who leave voluntarily receive 50% rather than 70% of their wages while unemployed. Because of the depressed job market, the lower rate would impose a severe hardship on anyone who volunteered to resign.

Gruen visualized the problem as an Evaporating Cloud, which looked something like the cloud in Exhibit 3-13. When the problem is defined as a cloud, the conflict that seems to be preventing a solution is immediately apparent. In this case, the conflict was that to do the best he could for employees, he would have to both file and not file for bankruptcy. The usual (non-TOC) response is to adopt a compromise solution, such as keep all of the employees on the payroll

Exhibit 3-13
The Employment Cloud—Company Q

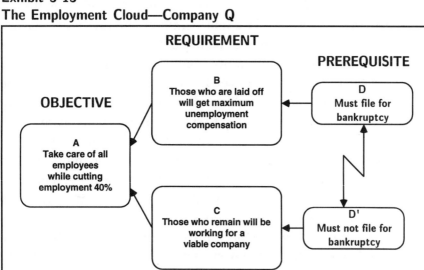

for a bit longer and then ask for voluntary resignations. However, the TOC approach is to resolve the problem by breaking one of the assumptions—that is, one of the arrows—so that the conflict no longer exists. Quite often, this approach involves stepping outside of the usual frame of reference.

In this case, Gruen broke the arrow connecting B and D. That is, he attacked the assumption that it is necessary to file for bankruptcy in order to have employees receive maximum unemployment compensation. He did it by asking everyone in the company (including himself) to agree to resign voluntarily if necessary. He then went to the unemployment office and placed his cards on the table. He said his choice was basically between filing for bankruptcy and shutting down the company altogether or accepting the voluntary resignation of some of the workers. However, the latter alternative was unpalatable because of the lower unemployment compensation for voluntary resignations. Gruen asked the civil servant at the unemployment office whether he would like to have 50 unemployed people drawing 70% of their wages or 20 people resigning voluntarily but also drawing 70% of their wages, with the other 30 people fully and gainfully employed and paying taxes. The civil servant saw the point and granted an exemption.

While this win-win solution undoubtedly seems clever, it may not be so clear what role the cloud really played in arriving at the solution. Our observations of this and other uses of the Evaporating Cloud technique lead us to believe that it has two main advantages. First, it focuses creative energy where it will do the most good—in breaking at least one of the assumptions underlying the presumed conflict. Second, the technique does not allow people to give up easily when confronted with a seemingly difficult conflict. While not everyone believes as Eli Goldratt does that every cloud can be evaporated, most people who have been introduced to the technique have seen enough examples of its power to be convinced that they should persevere and they should be creative.

After laying this groundwork for a partial reduction in the workforce, Gruen was pleasantly surprised to find that the employees who were laid off were very understanding and accepting. He says that on the day when he notified employees they would be laid off, "I left home feeling terrible and came home feeling happy."

However, to solve the fundamental problem, it was necessary to increase throughput as well as to cut operating expenses. Because of the new conditions in the market, Gruen felt that he had to drop his prices in order to get any sales. Recall that Company Q was selling high-end machines in a market that had gone downscale due to the recession. However, if he dropped prices, it would be difficult to raise them again in the future and if he did succeed in raising prices in the future, today's sales at distressed prices would cannibalize future sales at higher prices. Gruen visualized the problem as another cloud that looked something like the one in Exhibit 3-14.

In this cloud, Gruen felt the vulnerable assumption was represented by the arrow between D' and C, that is, the assumption that

Exhibit 3-14
The Pricing Cloud
Company Q

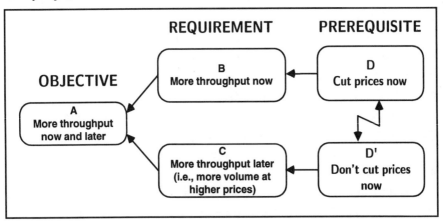

cutting prices now will reduce prices and sales volume in the future. The arrow was broken by stripping features (and their costs) off the company's high-end machines in such a way that the machines could be upgraded later by customers. Thus, customers could purchase more basic machines now at prices they could afford (and justify to higher authority) and then upgrade later as economic conditions improved. Like the earlier approach taken with the unemployment office, this was a win-win strategy. Both Company Q and its customers win.

At the time of our visit, the company had recovered from its 1992 crisis, and the order book had filled up enough to keep the company going for at least several more months.

Hofmans Forms Packing

Patrick Hoefsmit is one of the owners and managing director of three companies located in Rotterdam—an office supply and furniture merchandising company and two printing companies. The printing companies, which will be referred to collectively as Hofmans, make product labels, advertising brochures, computer and business forms, and folding cartons.

Almost all of Hofmans' products are mature and the printing industry generally has excess capacity, so competition is strong. Hofmans has less than a 5% market share except for one product in which it has a market niche of sorts. Due to a unique technology developed in-house, Hofmans can produce wraparound labels in small quantities economically, while the company's competitors will accept only orders for large quantities.

The printing shop is a job shop operation in which everything is made to order. Labor is about 60% of operating expenses and is effectively fixed. All lines currently have excess capacity except for wraparound labels.

When we first encountered Hoefsmit at a conference near Amsterdam in the fall of 1992, he was desperately seeking some way to avert the imminent collapse of the Hofmans printing company. When we visited Rotterdam one year later, the situation was much improved. The company was likely to wind up 1993 with a small profit despite a generally dismal economic outlook in Holland.

Like many others, Hoefsmit was introduced to TOC via *The Goal*, and he has given away many copies to managers in his firm and even to customers. He was in the first Jonah course offered by the Avraham Goldratt Institute that used formal trees. This 1991 course generally was considered to be a failure by both the participants and the Avraham Goldratt Institute. Hoefsmit also felt that the course was a disaster. The only formal training in TOC anyone else in the company has received was a one-day introductory workshop attended by six managers.

Hoefsmit says that in the past "we were really a cost-oriented company." They focused on minimizing conventionally computed unit costs, even though common sense told them that most such attempts wouldn't succeed. However, they lacked any other system for calculating the effects of actions on costs. He gave several examples. Hofmans had for many years been making document covers for Tim Voor Kantoor, the affiliated office supply company. These covers were made on an antiquated machine that had no other use. Cost figures that included labor and overhead indicated that the company was losing money on this product. Also, Tim Voor Kantoor could buy the product from one of Hofmans' competitors for almost exactly the same price it was paying Hofmans (a transfer price of cost minus 15%). Therefore, it was decided to kill the machine and the product and to acquire the covers from Hofmans' competitor. In retrospect Hoefsmit realizes this decision was a mistake. The machine had no other use and production of the covers was very simple. All that was required was for someone to refill the input hopper with materials occasionally. This job did not interrupt any other tasks and eliminating the product did not result in any reduction in labor costs. In essence, the only relevant costs were materials costs.

Instead of having Hofmans produce the document covers for just the cost of the materials, Tim Voor Kantoor now is purchasing them from a competitor at higher cost.

Another example of cost oriented thinking is the cost variance breakdown provided by the standard management information system software used in the Dutch printing industry. Quite often in printing, a particular job can be run on any one of several different machines, although the processing time and the "cost per hour" will differ across machines. The cost management software details the effects (according to the cost system) of switching a job from one machine to another. An example of this particular part of the variance report appears in Exhibit 3-15.

Exhibit 3-15
Variance Report—Hofmans Forms Packing

Assumptions: The standard for a particular job calls for it to be produced in three hours on a specific machine. The cost of using the machine is 150 Dutch guilders per hour. The job also could be produced on another, more expensive machine. Running the job on the alternative machine would require 2.5 hours but would cost 300 Dutch guilders per hour. The costs of using the machines consist almost entirely of fixed costs spread across expected usage.

If the alternative machine were used, the following variances would be generated:

"Pre"	"Real"	"Post"
3 hrs x 150 guilders per hr = 450 guilders	3 hrs x 300 guilders per hr = 900 guilders	2.5 hrs x 300 guilders per hr = 750 guilders

switch variance = 450 U　　efficiency variance = 150 F

commercial results = 300 U

Under this variance reporting system, if a job is switched to a more expensive machine, an unfavorable "switch" variance results. If a job is switched to a less efficient machine, an unfavorable efficiency variance results. The "commercial results" variance is the sum of the switch and efficiency variances. Therefore, if a job is switched to a more expensive and less efficient machine, three unfavorable variances result. Consequently, there is a great deal of resistance on the shop floor to moving jobs from "inexpensive" and "efficient" machines to more "expensive" and less "efficient" machines—even when the preferred machine is a bottleneck and the other machine is idle. Hoefsmit has discontinued efficiency reporting but says that he still is fighting this particular battle on the shop floor. Old habits are difficult to eradicate.

Hoefsmit provided another example of the distortions that result from attempting to minimize local measures of unit costs. Due to the highly competitive market in recent years, due date performance has become an important issue. The first attempt to compile statistics on due date performance revealed that only 58% of orders were being shipped on or before the due date. By simply directing the scheduler to improve due date performance, it went up to 85% but then did not get better. However, to be competitive, the due date performance would have to improve to the 98%-99% range. It seemed as if this improvement should be possible because the actual processing job for most jobs is about one day, and yet the lead time is about five weeks.

To understand the reasons for the poor due date performance, it is necessary to delve a little more deeply into the production process. Exhibit 3-16 provides a simplified flowchart for the printing plant. The first step in the production process is pre-press, which makes printing plates. If the customer already has approved the design and proofs, this stage can go fairly quickly. From pre-press, the job is routed to one of the printing machines. The printing machines have different capabilities—some jobs can be run on only one of the machines while there is a choice of machines for others. From the printing machines the job is routed to finishing if the job requires additional work such as die cutting. If not, the job is sent directly to packing and shipping.

Exhibit 3-16
Printing Plant Flowchart
Hofmans Forms Packing

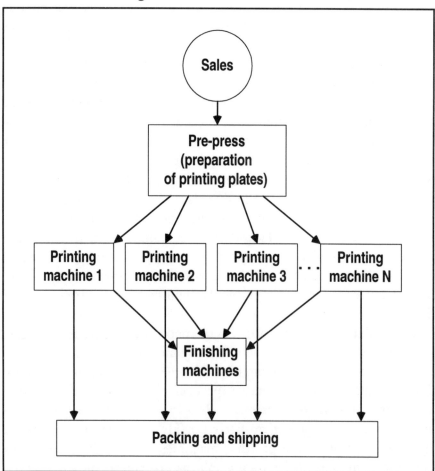

The plant planner schedules the plant based on due dates agreed on with sales. If the schedule is followed and there are no major unforeseen problems, the due dates should be met. However, Hoefsmit discovered that the printers often disrupt the schedule. If a printer sees that he won't have any work to do, he goes directly to pre-press and asks for more work. Pre-press responds by scanning the schedule for a job that can be run on the printer's machine. If such a job is found, it is released ahead of time. That is, pre-press prepares the printing plates before the schedule indicates they should be prepared and then releases the plates to printing prematurely. Basically, the plant is run to keep the presses operating, which creates several problems. The pre-press department works on jobs that are not yet due and neglects jobs that have higher priority, such as jobs that must go to the customer for proofing. Moreover, because materials are timed to arrive just-in-time, orders that are printed too soon must cannibalize materials from other orders. And when later jobs are released on schedule, they often are held up because required machines already are occupied processing prematurely released jobs.

Hoefsmit believes that this compulsion to keep the printing presses busy may have made sense in prior years when it was a sellers' market and due date performance was not particularly important. He suspected, however, that this policy might be causing much of the poor due date performance in the present buyers' market. He constructed a tree to analyze the problem. He predicted that if this disruption of the schedule was contributing to poor due date performance, he should observe both early and late orders arriving at shipping. Moreover, because late orders were being expedited routinely, he predicted that he would observe more early than late orders. This pattern is exactly what he found when he went to the data.

At the time of our visit, Hoefsmit was in the process of resolving this problem. Sales, planning, and pre-press were being asked to agree to a prioritization of orders. Once that priority list is established, pre-press will be required to follow the schedule.

The scheduling system was also in the process of revision at the time of our visit. Due dates and bills of materials and activities will be used to predict the existence of bottlenecks—that is, a resource whose capacity is insufficient to allow all orders to be delivered on time. If there is a bottleneck, the first line of defense is to off-load some of the work scheduled for the bottleneck onto nonbottleneck resources. If that action doesn't eliminate the due date problem, overtime is added. If that's not enough, sales is asked to go back to the customer for an adjustment of the due date.

Hoefsmit says that most of the constraints, such as in the examples given above, are the result of bad policies. Occasionally there are physical bottlenecks. For example, there were two very similar machines sitting next to each other—one is a three-color press and the other is a one-color press. The three-color press, which could handle one, two, or three colors, was a bottleneck whereas the one-color press had excess capacity. To break this bottleneck, the one color press was upgraded to a two-color press, and two-color work was off-loaded onto this press from the three-color machine. Hoefsmit figures that this investment should pay back in under two years just in overtime savings on the three-color press alone—not to mention the increase in throughput.

While TOC tends to emphasize increasing throughput over cutting operating expenses, Hoefsmit believes a TOC orientation also has helped him save money. He uses TOC principles to evaluate proposals for new equipment. For example, he was given a proposal for an expensive new jig for holding knife blades on a cutting machine. This jig would have saved considerable setup time and consequently would have increased the amount of time the machine is available for actual production. Standard setup cost calculations based on the cost of tying up expensive machine time indicated this was a super investment. However, this machine was not a bottleneck, the new jig was not needed to satisfy a customer requirement, and it would not have saved any operating expenses. Therefore, Hoefsmit concluded that there were no real benefits to making the investment and it was rejected.

We received mixed signals concerning the usefulness of the formal Thinking Process. Hoefsmit said despite the poor training he received in the Jonah course, he initially wanted to try doing everything with trees. However, he eventually came to the conclusion that the old way of doing things was almost always faster and less difficult but never as effective.

> The terrible thing is that you can't go around proudly spreading the news of your discoveries, but you have to use the buy-in or Socratic approach to give your people the chance to figure it out by themselves. Reread *The Goal* and try to be a Jonah and not an obnoxious wiseguy. But the good thing about using TOC is that you can be more distant from day-to-day problems and concentrate more on their causes. You also get more confident about your common sense.

On the other hand, trees have been used successfully on several occasions for difficult decisions involving drastic changes. Hoefsmit worked with Eli Goldratt on a plan to escape from very serious financial problems facing the printing company in the fall of 1992. An edited version of Hoefsmit's Current Reality Tree is presented in Exhibit 3-17. This tree is different from the usual current reality tree. Instead of starting with a set of undesirable effects and then connecting them in such a way that a core problem becomes apparent, the current reality tree was basically just a device to communicate to Goldratt why Hoefsmit believed he needed a new market in a hurry. In essence, Hoefsmit already had identified the core problem—"we don't have any new markets and don't have the time or money to develop any."

The first step in the plan was to identify an existing product for which new markets could be developed. Goldratt asked Hoefsmit about his markets and after Hoefsmit had mentioned everything else, he got around to wraparound labels, which Hoefsmit said was

Exhibit 3-17
Current Reality Tree
Hofmans Forms Packing

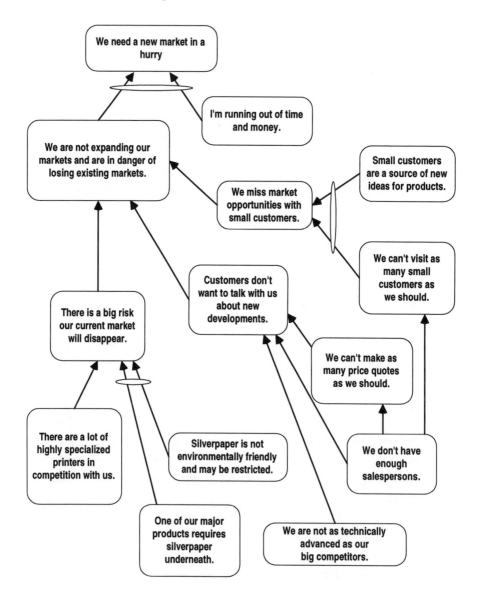

such a small market that it didn't really matter. Goldratt then challenged Hoefsmit to figure out how to make a gold mine out of wraparound labels. Hoefsmit at first thought it was almost a joke, but Goldratt's argument was that if you can figure out how to make a gold mine out of such an unpromising market, you can do it even more easily for other markets.

The complete action plan with all of its trees is far too detailed to present in its entirety here. Hofmans has a unique capability for producing wraparound labels—the company can produce them more economically in small lots than any competitor because of equipment Hofmans has developed in-house. Moreover, this line had excess capacity. To give a flavor for the depth and detail of the plan, an edited portion of the Prerequisite Tree is presented in Exhibit 3-18. The injection "Wraparound labels are a gold mine" is at the top. The tree contains all of the apparent obstacles to implementation and how those obstacles will be dealt with. The means of dealing with the obstacles are called intermediate objectives. The Prerequisite Tree should be read from top to bottom as follows: In order to have wraparound labels as a gold mine it is necessary to have customers who are willing and enthusiastic to place orders (entity 1). While this statement is true, there are several obstacles that may get in the way of having willing and enthusiastic customers. Someone is likely to object that the company doesn't have the capacity to make more labels (entity 4A), customers won't want to listen (entity 3A), or it would be too difficult to find customers who might be interested in ordering more wraparound labels (entity 2A). Each of these obstacles can be overcome if the intermediate objectives that appear immediately below them are realized. At this point, it is not necessary to know how these intermediate objectives will be realized, it is just important to note what they are. For example, the person constructing the trees may have no idea how the companies that make the wraparound labelling machines will be induced to supply Hofmans with their customer lists (entity 2), but

Exhibit 3-18
Prerequisite Tree—Hofmans Forms Packing

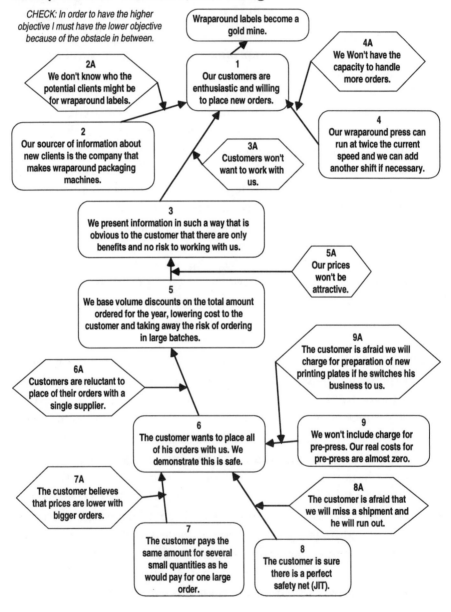

CHECK: In order to have the higher objective I must have the lower objective because of the obstacle in between.

Wraparound labels become a gold mine.

2A
We don't know who the potential clients might be for wraparound labels.

1
Our customers are enthusiastic and willing to place new orders.

4A
We Won't have the capacity to handle more orders.

2
Our sourcer of information about new clients is the company that makes wraparound packaging machines.

3A
Customers won't want to work with us.

4
Our wraparound press can run at twice the current speed and we can add another shift if necessary.

3
We present information in such a way that is obvious to the customer that there are only benefits and no risk to working with us.

5A
Our prices won't be attractive.

5
We base volume discounts on the total amount ordered for the year, lowering cost to the customer and taking away the risk of ordering in large batches.

9A
The customer is afraid we will charge for preparation of new printing plates if he switches his business to us.

6A
Customers are reluctant to place of their orders with a single supplier.

6
The customer wants to place all of his orders with us. We demonstrate this is safe.

9
We won't include charge for pre-press. Our real costs for pre-press are almost zero.

7A
The customer believes that prices are lower with bigger orders.

8A
The customer is afraid that we will miss a shipment and he will run out.

7
The customer pays the same amount for several small quantities as he would pay for one large order.

8
The customer is sure there is a perfect safety net (JIT).

if they do, then the obstacle of not knowing who the potential customers are would be overcome.

The point of the Prerequisite Tree is to identify the major obstacles (entities 2A, 3A, 4A, 5A, 6A, 7A, 8A, and 9A) and the steps or intermediate objectives (entities 2, 3, 4, 5, 6, 7, 8 and 9) required to overcome those obstacles. Following the completion of the Prerequisite Tree, a Transition Tree, or action plan, is drawn up. The Transition Tree looks very similar to a Current Reality Tree and contains the details required to implement the plan. In the Transition Tree the intermediate objectives are outcomes, or consequences, of actions taken by the planner. All of the intermediate objectives of the Prerequisite Tree, unless they already exist in reality, should be the outcomes of actions on the Transition Tree. So, for example, the Transition Tree would contain the details of how the planner intends to get the manufacturers of the wraparound labelling machines to divulge their client lists. (If attaining this intermediate objective seems to be an insurmountable task in itself, it then becomes the subject of a subsidiary analysis. That is, the intermediate objective is structured as the objective of a cloud. The cloud is evaporated with another injection, and so on.)

Skipping over the details of the rest of the rescue plan, its essence was to offer discounts to customers on cumulative volume over a year rather than for large individual orders. This method would permit customers to order in smaller quantities and to take deliveries more frequently—which the customers wanted—and still get volume discounts. By tying the customer to the company over the course of a year and by providing better service (smaller deliveries more frequently), Hoefsmit hoped to pick up substantial additional business. The plan was opposed internally because of the "costs" of the additional setups that would be required for smaller batches and simply because of inertia—such a policy had never been tried before. With respect to the first objection, Hoefsmit realized that setups were virtually free because the line was running at less than capacity. He persevered, entered into direct negotiations with some customers, and picked up so much additional business that the wraparound line now is running continuously and is a major contributor to profits. Modestly, he attributes this result as much to good fortune as to good planning.

Hoefsmit has had some success with using trees in meetings. He reports that on the few occasions when trees have been used to structure a meeting, the meetings have been shorter and have accomplished more. In a normal meeting without trees, people have a lot of excuses concerning why an idea is not practical, and they all feel they have to say something impressive. With trees, the meetings go somewhere.

Hoefsmit has the following suggestions for managers who want to try a group approach to solving problems with trees. First, build your own tree and then lay it aside. With this preparation, you will be better prepared to help the group overcome any impasses that develop. Then go to the group and start afresh. Ask the group to identify the undesirable effects so that they have ownership of the problem. Build the Current Reality Tree together. (Sometimes you will find that the tree built by the group is better than your own tree.) When the Current Reality Tree is completed and everyone agrees it is a reasonable representation of their reality, it is easy to convince people that the best procedure is to start from the bottom of the Current Reality Tree with the core problems. Starting this way focuses efforts on the real causes instead of on symptoms. Hoefsmit cautions that you should not let the group identify the core problem as something that is outside the group's control. Building trees should not be used as another excuse to point fingers; it should be a means of improving performance by changing what the group itself does.

While Hoefsmit was disappointed with his Jonah training and is skeptical concerning how often trees are a practical tool, he uses trees occasionally for particularly important problems, and he is committed to using other TOC approaches on a routine basis in his company. He calls his accounting staff the "history department" and says he believes people in his company only need throughput, operating expense, and asset data to determine the financial consequences of most day-to-day decisions.

Kent Moore Cabinets

Kent Moore is the owner and president of Kent Moore Cabinets (KMC), a custom cabinetmaker located in Texas. KMC builds cabinets primarily for new construction contractors in Bryan/College Station, Austin, Houston, and Dallas. KMC has built a reputation for quality, service, and quick response and dominates the Houston market but has less than 20% of the Austin and Dallas markets. Competition in the industry is fierce.

Everything at KMC is made to order. The Texas housing market is extremely seasonal with 70% of sales occurring from May through October. During this period KMC operates at capacity. In contrast, during the slow winter period there is a tremendous amount of surplus capacity.

Kent Moore became interested in TOC as a result of reading *The Goal.* He subsequently attended a Jonah course in January 1990. In addition to Moore, all top five managers at KMC are Jonahs. *The Goal* is required reading for all manufacturing team leaders, sales, drafting, and office personnel. They all have attended a two-day course in TOC principles. In the slower winter months, line people are trained in the Thinking Process. All of the managers use the formal Thinking Process, and all agree that TOC has changed everyone's job.

Moore says that "in the past we were sales and cost driven; now we are profit driven. I used to have monthly meetings where we would review the production efficiency reports and sales reports and beat each other up and then go back and do the same thing the next month. Now we don't even print those reports." Moore sees a dramatic improvement evidenced by substantial increases in net profit. In the past, each manager acted to solve his or her immediate problem without sufficient regard for the other managers' problems.

Management has refocused the company using the TP, which focuses group planning, identifies core problems and potential conflicts, and builds consensus. Internal reporting, production work flow, incentive compensation and market strategy all have changed. Previously, production management focused on local efficiency reporting that measured square feet of cabinet built per labor dollar for each department. The result of emphasizing this local measure of efficiency was lots of work-in-process, seasonal layoffs, and a 40-hour production cycle time. Since implementing TOC, production cycle time has been reduced to 12 hours, the company has no seasonal layoffs, and work-in-process inventory is limited to the planned buffer in front of the constraint.

KMC has five production departments in a job shop arrangement: the cutting department cuts all door and cabinet parts; the door lay-up department glues the door panels; the door shaping department sizes, shapes, and sands the door panel; the cabinet assembly department assembles the stiles and rails; and the final assembly department attaches the doors, inspects the finished cabinet, and prepares the product for shipping.

Prior to TOC, door panels, stiles, and rails were all cut at the same time, and the parts were released to the door lay-up department and the cabinet assembly department simultaneously. The door lay-up department was the bottleneck, so the other parts would accumulate in front of the cabinet assembly area waiting for the door panels to be finished. A variety of operating problems are detailed in Exhibit 3-19, which is an edited version of a Current Reality Tree prepared by John Trcalek, the vice president of production. An edited version of an associated Future Reality Tree appears in Exhibit 3-20.

As a consequence of such analysis, the work flow was reorga-

Exhibit 3-19
John Trcalek's Current Reality Tree

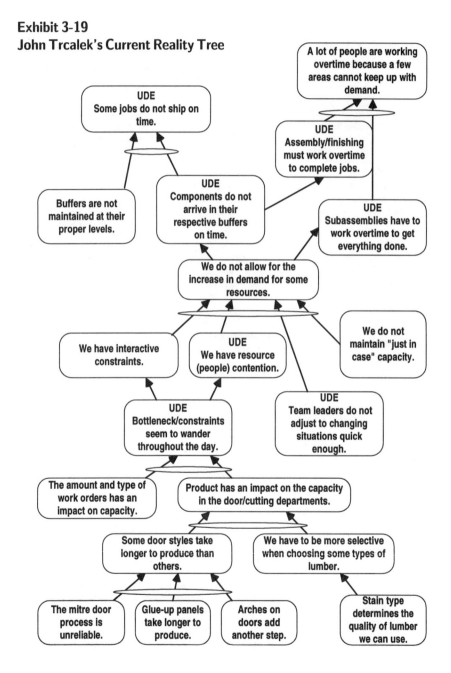

Exhibit 3-20
Kent Moore's Current Reality Tree

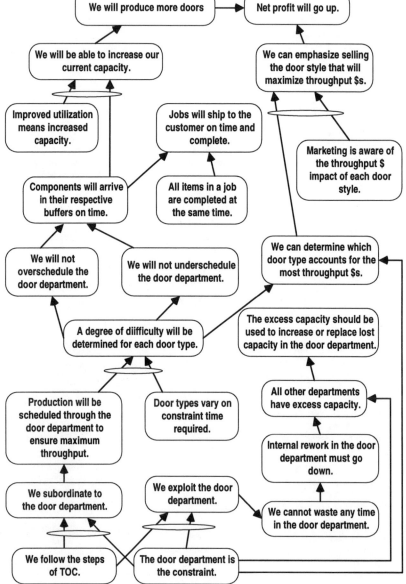

nized, and the door lay-up department became the drum for DBR scheduling. Door parts are cut first and a buffer of door parts is maintained in front of the bottleneck, which is the door lay-up department. After door panels are glued, a work order job label for the door is attached to the door panel. The glued door panel is sized and shaped, the edges are sanded, and it is moved to the chop saw where the stiles and rails are cut to match the door panel, according to the instructions on the work order job label. The door is then ready for final assembly.

Moore describes TOC as going against the grain of standard cost accounting practice. "Under our old efficiency reporting and measuring, we thought that running 100 parts across a machine in an hour costs half as much as running 50 parts an hour. But if you don't immediately need those 100 parts you haven't done any good, you've just created a pile of parts—not throughput."

Another example of ignoring conventional cost accounting practice is KMC's decision to sometimes substitute CNC router raised panel doors for flat panelled plywood doors. Raised panel doors do not go through the bottleneck, which is the door lay-up department. Therefore, by making this substitution during busy periods, KMC can handle more orders. KMC's customers are willing to allow the substitution because the market perceives the raised panel as an upgrade. The raised panel doors require more time to machine and use a sophisticated and expensive router, so traditional cost analysis would not have supported this action. KMC, on the other hand, views this work as essentially free because the machining is done on nonbottleneck machines and the router otherwise would be idle.

In 1991, Kent Moore identified several core problems using the formal Thinking Process. An edited version of one of his Current Reality Trees is presented in Exhibit 3-21, and an edited version of one of his Future Reality Trees, in Exhibit 3-22. One core problem identified as the result of such analysis was the seasonal building cycle. Although this tree is not presented, Kent Moore created a

Exhibit 3-21
Kent Moore's Current Reality Tree

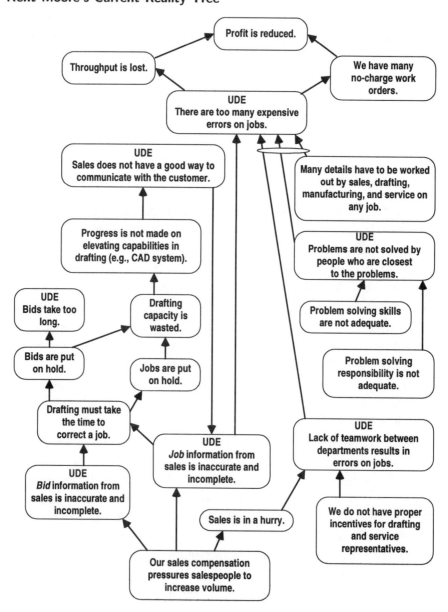

CRT and identified Undesirable Effects such as employee layoffs, low morale, loss of trained personnel, and negative cash flow in the trough and high work-in-process inventory, overtime, and poor on-time delivery in the peak.

KMC's success in the winter of 1993 was the result of a change in marketing strategy designed to overcome this seasonality problem. During 1992 KMC planned and implemented a market segmentation strategy to seek discount business and to target cabinet dealers in Florida. The Florida building season is opposite to the Texas building season, and by using dealers to sell and service the product, KMC need only deliver finished goods to the dealers. Previously KMC believed that they could not discount in the winter months because they already were losing money during those months. Their previous method of allocating all manufacturing costs to the product led them to conclude that they needed to charge higher prices in the winter. The shift to TOC thinking has allowed them to leverage off their unused fixed capacity in the winter and secure a base dealer business. The winter of 1993 was the first in which KMC has experienced a positive cash flow.

The vice president of finance, Charles Rinehart, says he has an entirely different perspective because of TOC. Credit policies are now more lenient in the slow months and much tighter in the busy season. Any bad debt during peak summer months, when the constraint is inside the plant, is a loss of throughput and cannot be regained, while a bad debt loss in the trough is just the raw material cost. One of Rinehart's first Trees analyzed KMC's cash flow problem. Aside from the seasonality mentioned above, Rinehart also identified the undesirable effects of generating "no-charge work orders" and "add-on work orders." These problems are discussed below.

KMC uses an in-house sales force. A customer places a potential order with a salesperson who turns it over to drafting for drawings and a bid. The salesperson reviews the drawings and the bid with the customer, and if the customer places the order, the drawings are re-

**Exhibit 3-22
Kent Moore's Future Reality Tree**

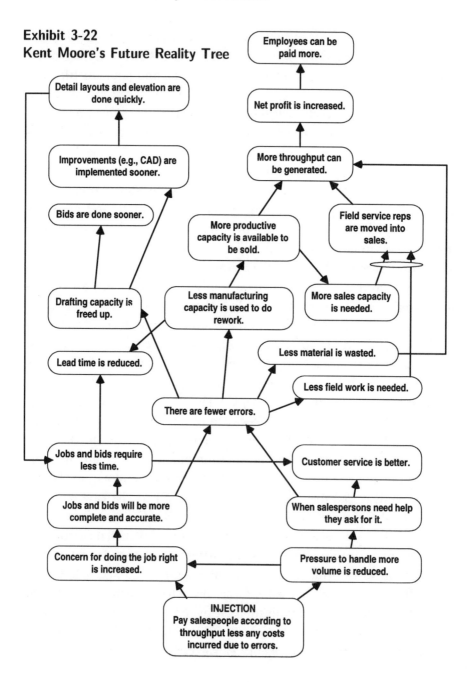

leased to production. The completed cabinets are delivered by company trucks and installed at the customer job site by outside contract laborers.

A company service representative is assigned to each salesperson to take care of customer complaints and errors in installation or design. If an error cannot be corrected in the field, a no-charge work order is written and contract labor is dispatched to pick up the cabinets to return to the factory. These work orders greatly erode the profit margins on jobs because contract labor, freight, and rework costs can be considerable. In addition to any out-of-pocket costs, rework during the busy season reduces throughput if it requires the use of the bottleneck, and it erodes the protective capacity of nonconstraint resources.

In addition, KMC had trouble collecting on receivables for add-on work orders that result from changes initiated by the contractor or homeowner after the cabinets have been delivered. The inability to collect add-on work orders consistently led to accounts receivable writeoffs and accounts receivables aging with outstanding receivables in the 60-day column and beyond. Although the delinquent receivables were a small percentage of the total accounts receivable balance, customer accounts with delinquent balances past 60 days render the entire customer receivable ineligible as collateral for short-term bank borrowing—a serious problem.

The Current Reality Tree in Exhibit 3-21 identifies inappropriate incentive compensation as the core problem leading to no-charge work orders. Prior to TOC, the sales force was paid a commission based on gross sales dollars. The service representatives and drafting personnel were salaried. Neither of these compensation policies aligned incentives with the goals of the company. The first change was to give salespersons a small bonus (less than $250) at the end of the month if none of their customers' accounts were 60 days past due. This minor change decreased writeoffs by 33%, and the average days outstanding dropped from 43 days to 35 days.

The second change was aimed at reducing the frequency of the sorts of errors that lead to no-charge work orders. The most common errors were specification errors on the part of the salesperson, design errors in drafting, or errors not corrected in the field by the service representative. To reduce these errors and build a more integrated team, the draftsmen and service representatives were put on commission along with the salespersons, and the basis for sales commissions was changed from gross sales to throughput dollars (defined as sales less raw materials and contract labor). The salesperson receives a base commission of 11% of throughput dollars. However, this commission rate is reduced by no-charge work orders. If the no-charge work order dollars are x% of sales dollars, the commission rate falls from 11% to 11%-x%. Thus, no-charge work orders can have a dramatic impact on compensation. Under this new compensation scheme, no-charge work orders as a percentage of sales fell 38%. In addition, contract labor returns of cabinets to the plant and reinstallation to correct no-charge work order problems were reduced from an average of 1.4% of sales dollars to .4% of sales dollars.

The third change to the incentive compensation plan allows salespersons to adjust prices on add-on work orders and one-time custom jobs, both of which are much less price sensitive than usual orders. Salespersons receive 40% of any excess over standard throughput dollars, so this new plan gives them powerful incentives to price these jobs at a premium and to land the sale. The program has encouraged salespersons to look for high margin jobs—especially during the trough when their incomes otherwise would decline. The previous gross sales incentive method led sales continually to seek large dollar jobs with contractors, regardless of the margins. The current incentive plan encourages salespersons to increase company net profit and better aligns sales, drafting, and service with the company's goals. Overall, it is estimated that these various changes in the compensation program have increased the company's net income by more than 4% of gross sales dollars.

The president of the company credits TOC with his company's turnaround and success. In 1988, KMC was in serious financial distress. Since 1988 KMC has nearly doubled its sales revenue without adding additional space or personnel and with dramatic bottom line results. All of KMC's managers have been with Moore for seven or more years and are convinced that TOC is not just another fad.

Notes

1. It is worthwhile to note that throughput as measured by Baxter-Lessines would be different from throughput as measured by the parent company. The reason is that as far as Baxter-Lessines is concerned, its price is standard full absorption product cost. However, as far as the parent company is concerned, the price is the ultimate selling price of the product. Through no fault of Baxter-Lessines, this difference may result in some suboptimal decisions when viewed from the standpoint of the entire company. We saw no evidence of this, but the possibility exists.

2. Another situation in which a company computes full cost data as a means of estimating what its competitors will bid is reported in James T. Mackey and Vernon Hughes, "Decision-Focused Costing at Kenco," *Management Accounting*, May 1993, pp. 22-26.

3. A similar approach to pricing is reported in the Wharton Manufacturing Company (A) case in *Cases from Management Accounting Practice*, Volume 8, edited by James T. Mackey, Institute of Management Accountants, 1992, Montvale, New Jersey, pp. 43-47.

4. Shigeo Shingo, *Modern Approaches to Manufacturing Improvement: The Shingo System*, edited by Dr. Alan Robinson, Productivity Press, Cambridge, 1990, p. 80.

4 Further Observations and Conclusions _____

This chapter is based on our personal opinions and is more speculative than the material in the earlier chapters. We begin with the Thinking Process and proceed with a variety of observations concerning the uses and implications of the Theory of Constraints.

The Thinking Process

The formal Thinking Process is potentially a powerful tool for identifying and implementing solutions to just about any problem. It can be used to attack small problems or big problems. It can be applied to strategic problems in a multinational Fortune 500 company or to mundane family problems such as the conditions under which a teenager can have access to a car. The scope of an analysis using the Thinking Process is determined solely by the scope of the problems (Undesirable Effects) the analyst wants to tackle. Unlike TQM, where the emphasis is on continuous incremental improvement, the Thinking Process can yield breakthrough insights and solutions. However, it also can be used as an incremental tool in a TQM program. In particular, a Current Reality Tree analysis can be used instead of a fishbone analysis. In our opinion the Current Reality Tree is a far more sophisticated tool and is likely to produce better insights.

Given the apparent potential of the Thinking Process, we were disappointed to see that it was used infrequently. It was used more or less routinely in a few places, but at most sites it got almost no use. While nearly everyone we talked to believes that the payoff from using the TP may be very big, very few people were willing to invest the time and effort to actually use it on a routine basis. The reason is evident—a steep learning curve is associated with the TP. Very few of the managers we met felt that they had yet reached the point on the curve where the benefits of routinely using the TP outweighed the costs. To some degree, this view is due to the novelty of the TP. It is a complex technique that has been developed over the last several years and is still evolving. Consequently, very few of the managers we talked with felt that they had received adequate training in the technique. Those who have taken the Jonah course more recently were much more satisfied with the adequacy of the training and were somewhat more likely to use the techniques actively. Some did feel that too much time is devoted now in the Jonah course to the Thinking Process and not enough time to more traditional TOC issues such as Throughput Accounting and Drum-Buffer-Rope scheduling.

We question whether most people can be taught to use the Thinking Process independently on a routine basis. There is some controversy within the Avraham Y. Goldratt Institute concerning this issue. Now that the training materials have been improved, Eli Goldratt firmly believes that anyone can master the TP. Others are less optimistic. We believe there are some people who can learn the TP and apply it successfully on a routine basis after two weeks of training, but we suspect that most people cannot. We also suspect that even with unlimited training some people will never feel comfortable with the technique. If we are correct, it is unfortunate.

We agree with Eli Goldratt that the best solutions are those invented by the people who must implement them. Those who are closest to the problems are likely to have the best intuition about them and certainly would have more of the relevant facts at hand.

Inventing a solution provides a powerful psychological impetus to see the solution through to successful completion. Based on our interviews, we are pessimistic, however, about how many people can really master the TP enough to use it independently.

One company we visited got around this human limitation by using facilitators. They were staff persons who received more intensive training in the TP than others and who were available to help with analyses as the need arose. This approach seemed to be working quite well. To be successful, a facilitator should be comfortable with and fully conversant in the TP, analytical, self-effacing, and trusted. Also, the top of the organization must be fully committed to using the TP in problem solving. Without that commitment, very few people will bother to use it.

Is TOC a "production thing"?

The emphasis at the Avraham Y. Goldratt Institute has shifted toward the Thinking Process with its generic approach to problem solving and away from concrete operational matters such as Throughput Accounting and Drum-Buffer-Rope scheduling. Nevertheless, we believe that tremendous potential for applying these more concrete and specific techniques still exists—particularly in job shops with unbalanced capacities. The five-step method for managing constraints remains a very simple and yet powerful tool for continuous improvement. Application of these ideas from *The Goal* (and complementary techniques such as single minute exchange of dies at bottleneck resources) to the typical job shop situation can quickly yield substantial improvements in turnover, due date performance, cycle time, throughput, and profits—and at virtually no cost.

There are very real dangers, however, when TOC is confined to the shop floor and is not adopted throughout a business. Production is usually able to improve its own processes to the point where the constraint shifts to the market. We found this pattern over and over again in the companies we visited. At that point some other function in the organization—probably marketing—will have to improve or profits will stagnate. If that other function does not want to change or does not know what to change or how to change, then the entire organization will stagnate. Goldratt warns:

> In such a situation, we can expect that the pressure of the organization to continue to improve will be channeled into the other two avenues which are still open—reduction of Inventory and Operating Expense. But let's not fool ourselves, only one avenue is actually open. The magnitude by which we can reduce our total Inventory is very limited... [A]ll the pressure to improve the organization's performance will eventually become focused on the only open avenue—reduction of Operating Expense. Let's face it— what is the real meaning of reducing Operating Expense? In real life terminology, it is just another name for laying-off people. ... Who are the people most likely to be impacted by those layoffs? Most probably not the ones in the function that is now the constraint of the company. They are already overwhelmed with work and everybody is well aware of it. No, the pressure will be directed to the functions that seem to have excess manpower. Those are exactly the functions that made the most dramatic improvements. ... [I]n the end, we will be forced to punish the ones who improved.[1]

This action would, of course, effectively kill any chance of further improvement in the organization for quite a long time.

These arguments apply as well to TQM and other improvement programs. Such improvement programs often uncover excess capacity and when improvements in profits stop or don't materialize, the pressure becomes intense to eliminate that excess capacity. And because the excess capacity almost certainly will be in precisely those areas where there has been the most improvement, those areas will likely be the first to feel the axe.

Goldratt also argues that the pilot project approach to TOC does not usually work—particularly when the pilot project is the production area. Even when there are very impressive results from the pilot project, the "not invented here" syndrome rears its ugly head. Goldratt argues that when implementation is already in place in production, "all our efforts to convince marketing and engineering didn't even make a dent. The emotional resistance, which already exists, prevents almost any meaningful dialogue. . . . The lesson today is loud and clear. Before any function can go on an ego trip, demonstrating and waving results (and by that digging its own grave)—before any function can start individual improvements, all functions should decide together on a common way."[2]

These claims could be dismissed easily as consulting hype designed to sell more training courses. However, the effects predicted by Goldratt were quite evident at the two sites we visited where Jonahs were confined to manufacturing. At one of the sites, inventories had been reduced dramatically, reject rates were way down, lead times had been cut by a third, on-time delivery had improved by more than 50%, and operating expenses were down significantly even though output was up. However, the production managers were not supported by top management, who felt that decision and management styles suited to marketing and top management were incompatible with TOC and the Thinking Process. Consequently, there was considerable tension in the organization and most of the Jonahs had left.

At another site, a wholly owned subsidiary of a large corporation, we were told that the former vice president of manufacturing was fired as a direct result of unfavorable manufacturing variances caused by implementation of TOC. Cycle time had been reduced by 70%, work-in-process inventories had been cut by 80%, and stock-outs had been virtually eliminated. However, we were told that the unfavorable efficiency variances that resulted from liquidating excess inventories and from cutting batch sizes had led to the sacking of the vice president.

In a well-functioning job shop, volume and efficiency variances should be unfavorable at the nonbottlenecks. On average, nonbottlenecks should be used at less than capacity and small lot sizes should be the rule. Indeed, favorable volume and efficiency variances at the nonbottlenecks are likely to signal impending problems. Unfavorable efficiency variances also may be reported at the bottleneck as less efficient processes are brought on-line to increase throughput. Therefore, any job shop manager who embarks on TOC without first getting agreement with superiors concerning the appropriate interpretation of volume and efficiency variances is doomed to a great deal of frustration and ultimate failure.

Goldratt simply echoes the theme that is repeated over and over again in the TQM literature. Change must be supported fully by top management, and the process for change must be diffused throughout the business unit. On the bright side, this statement does not necessarily mean that the top management of the entire company must be behind TOC. It does mean, however, that the level at which TOC is implemented should be an autonomous business unit evaluated based on its own operating profit.

TOC and cost cutting

An advantage of TOC is that it can simplify the annual planning process. Only the work loads and capacity at the bottlenecks need to be known with any precision. Consequently, fairly large errors in setup and processing time standards at nonbottlenecks can be tolerated without any problem. However, when excess capacity is revealed at the nonbottlenecks, managers may be tempted to try to save money by trimming away unused capacity. Some of this trimming may be a good idea, but there is a big difference between excess capacity and protective capacity. Trimming into the protective capacity can have very unfortunate repercussions because it is required to buffer the constraint from unforeseen events and therefore protects throughput and profits. We did not notice any problems in this area in our interviews, but it is a potential danger if the benefits of protective capacity are not well appreciated.

In general, TOC does not provide much guidance for efforts at cost reduction; indeed the TOC literature is generally hostile toward cost reduction, for several reasons:

- Many cost reduction efforts in the past really have focused on reducing unit costs by spreading fixed costs over more units. If the additional volume is not sold, it results in larger inventories without any real benefit.

- Cost reductions often take the form of across-the-board cuts that create problems and that have little lasting effect on spending.

- Real operating improvements that uncover excess capacity may be followed by personnel cuts. This action can lower morale and may make it very difficult to continue improving in the future.

Nevertheless, it seems to be undeniable that there are opportunities in many organizations to improve processes and that these improvements can, under some circumstances, yield real and lasting cost savings in the form of reduced spending. Moreover, these opportunities are at least as likely to be at the nonbottlenecks as at the bottlenecks. In practice, we did not see any strong evidence that managers at TOC sites were neglecting these opportunities, although very few were involved in systematic programs such as TQM.

TOC versus ABC

The product strategies of companies involved in TOC can differ dramatically from those of companies that use activity-based costing. TOC typically uncovers capacity and provides production flexibility that makes more variety possible in the company's product offerings. Products invariably appear more profitable in a TOC shop than in a shop where product margins are computed using full costs. Providing that a new product with positive throughput does not use the constraint, it will appear attractive. Therefore, products will tend to proliferate in a TOC environment. ABC, on the other hand, can lead easily to a decrease in product offerings. A switch from a conventional costing system with volume-related allocation bases to an ABC system with batch or product level cost pools will shift costs from high-volume to low-volume products. The usual result is a "profitability map" that suggests low-volume products are losing money. If managers respond by dropping such products, the offerings of the company will shrink. Thus, TOC and ABC can have opposite effects on the variety of products offered by a company.

These differences in strategy can be traced back to differences in fundamental assumptions about the way costs behave. In TOC, it is assumed that almost all costs other than materials are fixed—that is, they ordinarily will not increase solely due to an increase in the volume of output. In the usual ABC implementation, it is assumed that all costs are variable in the sense that they are strictly proportional to activity. The activity might be the number of batches or the number of parts or whatever, but the assumption is that the costs assigned to a cost pool are strictly proportional to the activity used as an allocation basis for the cost pool.[3]

As discussed earlier, the TOC approach is very similar to variable costing except that the orthodox position in TOC is that direct labor is a fixed cost. As in variable costing, under TOC the impact of decisions on fixed costs is estimated on a case-by-case basis. In some decisions, fixed costs change and are relevant, but in others they do not change and are not relevant. In TOC the presumption appears to be even stronger than in variable costing that fixed costs are not relevant unless there is a good reason to believe that they are.

This idea has interesting implications for the behavior of overhead in TOC environments. In TOC it is usually assumed that product proliferation and increased volume have no appreciable effect on operating expenses. Therefore, no increase in operating expenses is budgeted automatically or authorized solely as a result of an increase in volume or the variety of product offerings. Managers at almost all of the sites we visited claimed that they had been able to reduce or keep operating expenses constant despite increased volume and variety. This fact is surprising given the assertions made in the ABC literature concerning the effects of volume and variety on overhead costs. We believe these companies have been able to hold the line on operating expenses simply by saying no to any increases. If more demands are placed on the existing overhead resources, there is no choice except to eliminate nonvalue-added activities. This is essentially the point made by Tom Johnson—managers should be concerned with improving processes rather than measuring how many resources are being consumed using existing inefficient processes.[4]

This approach works only so long as there is fat in the form of nonvalue-added activity in the overhead areas. Ultimately product proliferation and increasing activity are likely to create demands for additional overhead resources. At several companies, managers mentioned that increased activity and product varieties had created pressures to expand support staff. They spoke in terms of the constraint shifting from the shop floor to engineering or design. When this happens, TOC is able to cope with the situation without missing a beat. The constraint can be elevated by acquiring more capacity in engineering just as a machine constraint can be elevated by purchasing another machine.

The floating bottleneck problem

One of the most frequent questions we encounter from those who know something about TOC but who are skeptical about its usefulness is, "How does TOC cope with bottlenecks that constantly move around?" The answer is that no one can really cope with situations in which the constraint flits from one place to another apparently at random. One of the fundamental insights of TOC is that whether we like it or not, our success is determined largely by how we manage the constraints in the system. We can choose to manage the constraints or we can let them manage us. When the bottleneck floats at random from one work center or machine to another, chaos is inevitable. Due date performance, WIP inventory levels, through-put, cycle time, and so on will be determined by where the bottle-neck happens to be at the moment. To get control over operations, it is necessary to stabilize the location of the bottleneck. This is not to say that the location of the bottleneck can never change; however, ideally it should change only as the result of an explicit decision. Among other things, this statement implies that capacities at work centers should not be balanced. The ideal situation, as discussed ear-lier, is one in which the capacity at the bottleneck is sufficiently less than the capacities at the nonbottlenecks so that the nonbottlenecks can absorb disruptions without turning into bottlenecks.

In a nutshell, if you have a floating bottleneck, you have a funda-mentally chaotic situation—whether or not you attempt to apply TOC principles. The TOC solution is to unbalance the capacities so that one of the work centers is predictably the bottleneck and then protect the bottleneck with buffer inventories. The JIT solution is to drive all variation out of the system so that there are no disruptions and the flows remain perfectly smooth throughout the entire sys-tem. As a practical matter, the TOC solution is usually easier and quicker to implement, but both approaches can be used in concert.

Strategic implications of the bottleneck

When the constraint is a production bottleneck, there are major implications for pricing, product strategies, and control of operations. The contribution margin per unit of the constrained resource should have a major impact on what products are made and how they are priced. A product whose contribution margin per unit of the con-strained resource is too low should be de-emphasized. Prices on new and existing products should cover at least out-of-pocket costs plus opportunity costs (i.e., the contribution margin per unit of the con-strained resource for the marginal product). Because the contribu-tion margin per unit of the constrained resource will depend on the location of the bottleneck, and pricing and product mix decisions depend on the contribution margin per unit of the constrained resource, the inference is that the location of the bottleneck has strategic implications. Product mixes and prices can differ dramatically, depending on which work station happens to be the bottleneck. There is something troubling about this—especially because the location of the bottleneck can be nothing more than an historical accident. We didn't hear anyone say so at the sites we visited, but an explanation for a bottleneck could be, "The former owner didn't order a big enough heat treat furnace, so that's the bottleneck." Why should the company's strategy depend on this happenstance?

The question has two answers. The first is that, given the present situation, the company's product mix and pricing strategy should depend on whatever happens to be the bottleneck constraint—for whatever reason. The constraint is a fact of life. Ignoring it does not make it go away. The second answer is that, over time, the bottleneck is likely to change if management follows the five steps for managing constraints. Whenever a constraint is encountered, it should be exploited and then elevated. If it is elevated enough, it will no longer be the constraint. Some constraints are easier and less costly to elevate than others. And, stepping outside of the Theory of Constraints for a moment, an economist would add that a constraint should be elevated as long as the marginal benefit exceeds the marginal cost. In the process of elevating the constraint, the point may be reached at which the constraint shifts to another resource. However, it also can happen that the marginal benefit from elevating the constraint is less than the marginal cost before that point is reached. In such a situation, further improvement is blocked (at least temporarily). Therefore, there would be some tendency for bottlenecks to stabilize at work stations where the marginal costs of elevating the constraints exceed the marginal benefits.

Given that different companies have different capabilities, this situation would seem to imply that the bottleneck in a company is most likely to occur in the area where it is competitively the weakest. That is, the bottleneck is somewhat more likely to occur in the area where the company gets less marginal benefit per dollar of investment than its competitors. For strategic purposes, one can argue that this point is precisely where the company should concentrate its improvement efforts—in the area where it is weakest relative to its competitors. TOC accomplishes this objective if, as we argue, the company's weakest area is the constraint. Some caution is in order. The company must be careful not to lose its competitive edge in those areas where it has an advantage. Nevertheless, one can argue that TOC will have a tendency to focus attention more or less automatically on the most important areas to improve from a strategic standpoint. Having said this, the strategic implications of constraints have not been fully explored. This issue currently is receiving attention at the Avraham Y. Goldratt Institute.

Conclusion

The Theory of Constraints is a remarkably coherent and logical framework for managing complex processes. It does not appeal to everyone and it has not always been applied successfully. As with other improvement programs, such as TQM, the failures probably outnumber the successes in the sense that the improvements fall short of expectations. Our sample was undoubtedly biased in favor of TOC. Our contacts for the study were made at two conferences attended by people who are likely to be more committed to TOC than the average. Moreover, all of those who participated in the study took the initiative to volunteer. Even with this self-selection bias in favor of TOC, on average, TOC was only moderately successful. It was extremely successful in perhaps a quarter of the companies we visited and had become a central focus for management, but in most of the other companies it was not being applied consistently. The relative lack of use in most of the companies did not seem to be due to lack of opportunities to apply TOC constructively. Some people just seem to take to TOC more naturally than others. The critical question is whether the top manager really believes in TOC and uses it consistently. If he or she does, the rest of the organization will usually follow—with varying levels of enthusiasm.

The accounting in TOC should be familiar territory to management accountants. While the terms used in TOC are different from those we commonly use, variable costing, use of scarce resources, and responsibility accounting have been topics in management accounting textbooks for decades. From a theoretical viewpoint, little in TOC is new to accounting. The difference is that some topics—particularly, use of scarce resources—are far more important than we thought and are given more prominence in TOC. The companies involved in TOC are different from most companies in that they actually put into practice much of the advice found in the textbooks. Surveys over the last several decades have revealed consistently that most companies do not follow many of the practices advocated in management accounting textbooks. Absorption costing routinely is used for internal decision making, corporate headquarters expenses are allocated to divisions in performance reports, product profitability calculations ignore constraints, and so forth. For those of us who teach management accounting, it is reassuring that an identifiable collection of companies practice what we preach.

What does the future hold for TOC? The most obvious applications are found in job shops, and managers of such shops will undoubtedly continue to mimic Alex Rogo's actions in *The Goal*. These efforts usually will be rewarded with almost immediate improvements in operations and in profits at virtually no cost. However, such efforts ultimately will lead to failure unless management outside of manufacturing is willing to embrace TOC or to evaluate manufacturing performance using TOC measures.

Looking beyond the elements of TOC found in *The Goal*, our crystal ball becomes murkier. The TP may be the most important intellectual achievement since the invention of calculus. On the other hand, it also may be a complete flop. It is just too early to tell. We saw some hopeful signs. Quite a few people who have been trained as Jonahs use parts of the TP on an occasional basis. However, very few have come even close to mastering the entire TP, and very few use it routinely. We believe this fact reflects the difficulty of mastering and using the technique rather than any inherent limitations in the technique itself. With time, as the TP is refined and people get more practice using it, we anticipate its being used much more widely and routinely. Indeed, educators outside of the Avraham Y. Goldratt Institute are now experimenting with teaching the TP at all levels from elementary to graduate school. It would be profoundly depressing if this noble experiment were ultimately to fail. The TP is nothing less than an attempt to get people to think through problems and their solutions logically and systematically.

Notes

1. Eliyahu M. Goldratt, *The Theory of Constraints*, North River Press, Croton-on-Hudson, N.Y., 1990, pp. 92-93.

2. Ibid., p. 96.

3. The only evidence to date on this issue indicates that overhead costs are less than proportional to activity and therefore overhead costs assigned to products under an ABC system are systematically overstated—perhaps by 40% or more. See Eric Noreen and Naomi Soderstrom, "Are Overhead Costs Strictly Proportional to Activity?," *Journal of Accounting and Economics*, January 1994, pp. 255-278.

4. H. Thomas Johnson, *Relevance Regained*, The Free Press, New York, 1992.

Appendix

Appendix: An Introduction to the Thinking Process_____

Introduction

This appendix is intended to be an introduction to the Thinking Process—an analytical tool developed by the Avraham Y. Goldratt Institute (AGI). While we cover all of the main elements of the Thinking Process, we omit many of the details. We seriously doubt that anyone could perform a complete analysis of a difficult problem after reading this summary. On the other hand, we hope that this appendix will give the reader a better feel for what the TP is all about.

In Chapter 2 we described the basic elements of the TP and indicated how they fit together. Exhibit A-1 reproduces the pivotal exhibit dealing with the Thinking Process from that chapter. A complete analysis begins with a list of Undesirable Effects that the preparer would like to eliminate. The Current Reality Tree is used to identify one or more core problems that apparently cause those Undesirable Effects. The immediate objective, or first step toward the solution, is the opposite of the core problem. If the objective seems impossible, an Evaporating Cloud is used to expose the underlying assumptions that make it appear beyond reach. An injection is a change that once implemented will change the environment in such a way that the assumptions in the Evaporating Cloud will no longer be valid. The

Exhibit A-1
The Roles of the Thinking Process Tools

What to change?	*What to change to?*	*How to change?*
Current Reality Tree	Evaporating Cloud	Prerequisite Tree
	Future Reality Tree	Transition Tree

Future Reality Tree is used to verify that the injection will eliminate the original Undesirable Effects without creating more problems. The Prerequisite Tree is used to identify obstacles to implementation of the injection. The Transition Tree is a detailed plan for overcoming those obstacles.

Thinking Process—Current Reality Tree

The process of building the Current Reality Tree usually begins with a list of symptoms, called "Undesirable Effects," or UDEs, in the jargon of the Thinking Process. (UDE is pronounced you-dee.) The problem is somehow to deduce from this list of Undesirable Effects a limited number of possible causes. For example, a manager at one of the sites we visited was concerned with problems in the stockroom and on the shopfloor. He had a long list of Undesirable Effects that became the basis for a large and complex Current Reality Tree.[1] To illustrate how a Current Reality Tree is constructed, we have extracted from his list of Undesirable Effects the six UDEs in Exhibit A-2 and will construct, using that list, an edited and abbreviated version of his Current Reality Tree.

Just as with a medical diagnosis, a single symptom is not very informative because it has too many possible causes. On the other hand, the diagnosis can become difficult if there are too many symptoms. In such a case, a doctor may suspect that more than one disease is afflicting the patient. The AGI has developed Guidelines for Building Current Reality Trees, reproduced in Exhibit A-3. Step 1 of

Exhibit A-2
List of Undesirable Effects (UDEs)

---

1. There is not enough space in the stockroom.
2. There is too much make-to-stock inventory.
3. Items pile up waiting to be stored in the stockroom.
4. One division takes another's parts on a first-come, first-served basis.
5. Cycle times are longer than necessary.
6. There is too much work-in-process.

---

the Guidelines recommends beginning with a list of five to 10 UDEs. (These Guidelines, like the rest of the Thinking Process, appear to be a mixture of pure logic and somewhat ad hoc rules developed through inspired trial-and-error.)

Step 2 of the Guidelines recommends directly connecting any UDEs that seem to be causally related, that is, one UDE is the cause of another UDE. This step has been carried out in Exhibit A-4. The manager who constructed this diagram believed that the items that were piling up waiting to be stored in the stockroom (UDE 3) and the excess inventories that result from making parts to stock (UDE 2) contribute significantly to the lack of space in the stockroom (UDE 1). Therefore, he connected them with arrows.

Step 3 of the Guidelines consists of building a complete causal road map that shows how all of the UDEs are consequences of a few root causes. We don't know the precise order in which the manager constructed the Current Reality Tree in the example we are using. Nevertheless, he might have followed the progression shown in Exhibits A-5 through A-9. We will walk through those exhibits in order to give a flavor for how the Thinking Process is used.

In Exhibit A-5, a cause is suggested for items piling up waiting to be stored in the stockroom (UDE 3). The suggested cause is that parts are delivered to the stockroom in large quantities and that delivery schedules do not match the rate of usage. This statement,

Exhibit A-3
Guidelines for Building Current Reality Trees
(reproduced with permission of the AGI)

Step 1. Make a list of between five and 10 Undesirable Effects (UDEs) that describe the area being analyzed, and subject each UDE to the Entity Existence Reservation.

Step 2. If you see an apparent connection between two or more UDEs, connect this "cluster" while scrutinizing* each entity and arrow along the way. Otherwise, choose one UDE at random and continue on to Step 3.

Step 3. Connect all other UDEs to the result of Step 2, scrutinizing* each entity and arrow along the way. Stop when all UDEs have been connected.

Step 4. Read the tree from the bottom up, scrutinizing* again each arrow and entity along the way. Make any necessary corrections.

Step 5. Ask yourself if the tree as a whole reflects your intuition about the area. If not, check each arrow for Additional Cause Reservations.

Step 6. Don't hesitate to expand your tree to connect other UDEs that exist but were NOT included in the original UDE list. DO NOT PERFORM THIS STEP UNTIL ALL THE ORIGINAL UDES ARE CONNECTED.

Step 7. Revisit the UDEs. Identify those entities in the tree which are negative on their own merit, even if the entity was not on the original list of UDEs or it requires that you expand the tree upwards one or two entities.

Step 8. Trim from your tree any entities that are not required in order to connect all of the UDEs.

Step 9. Present your tree to someone who will help you surface and challenge the assumptions captured within.

Step 10. Examine all entry points of the tree and decide which are the ones that you feel a desire to attack. Pick from them the one that contributes the most to the existence of the UDEs. If it doesn't impact at least 70% of the re-selected UDEs, add V-type connections.

* Scrutinize in accordance with the Categories of Legitimate Reservations (see Exhibit A-8).

Exhibit A-4
Constructing a Current Reality Tree (Part 1)

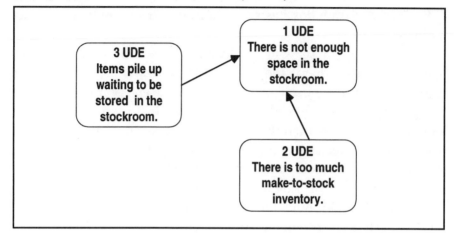

Exhibit A-5
Constructing a Current Reality Tree (Part 2)

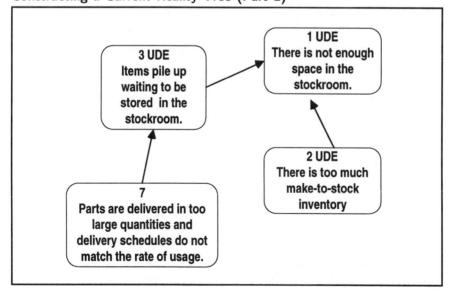

like the UDEs themselves, is enclosed in a box that contains a reference number. Each box containing a statement is called an "entity." The number in the box has no significance; it is simply a reference point.

The arrows in the Current Reality Tree are "sufficiency" arrows—the entity that is the source of the arrow is presumed to be a significant cause, by itself, of the entity at the end of the arrow. The connecting arrows are read in a specific way. If an arrow points from entity A to entity B, then the connection is read "if A, then B." Thus, the arrow connecting entity 7 with entity 3 is read "if parts are delivered to the stockroom in large quantities and delivery schedules do not match the rate of usage, then items pile up waiting to be stored in the stockroom." There may be additional reasons why items pile up in the stockroom, but entity 7 acting alone is presumed to be a significant cause of this phenomenon.

Continuing on with the process of building the Current Reality Tree, the preparer decided that the main reason why parts are delivered in too large quantities (entity 7) is that work orders are often larger than divisions' needs. This addition to the tree is displayed in Exhibit A-6. Indeed, the exhibit indicates that the fact that work orders are often larger than the divisions really need is the cause of many of the problems. This is progress, but one of the UDEs has yet to be linked to the others. Step 3 in the guidelines for building a Current Reality Tree requires that all the UDEs be connected. The remaining UDE is "One division takes another's parts on a first-come, first-served basis." The preparer has suggested a link between entity 8 and this UDE in Exhibit A-7.

The preparer has now reached the end of Step 3 in the Guidelines for Building Current Reality Trees listed in Exhibit A-3. All of the original UDEs have been connected. In Step 4, the preparer is supposed to read the tree from the bottom up, scrutinizing each arrow and entity along the way using the Categories of Legitimate Reservations listed in Exhibit A-8. For example, during the review of the tree, the preparer concluded that entity 11 is not sufficient in itself to cause entity 4. That is, the fact that the supplying division is often behind schedule does not by itself lead to the Undesirable Effect that one division takes another's parts. Something is missing from the tree. Therefore the preparer has fleshed out the tree in Exhibit A-9. Entities 9 and 10 have been added to the tree and a curious elliptical object is overlapping the arrows leading from entities 9 and 10 into entity 4. This object is what logicians call a

Exhibit A-6
Constructing a Current Reality Tree (Part 3)

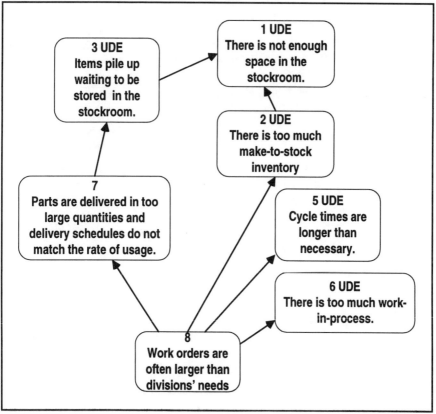

"logical AND" but is called by the less technical term "banana" in the Thinking Process. Because of this "banana," the relationship between entities 9, 10, and 4 should be read as follows: If inventory does not have divisional identity (entity 10) *and* there are often not enough parts available (entity 9), then one division takes another's parts on a first-come, first-served basis (entity 4). The banana means that you need both causes to get the effect. When arrows leading into an entity are not overlapped by a banana, it means that you will

Exhibit A-7
Constructing a Current Reality Tree (Part 4)

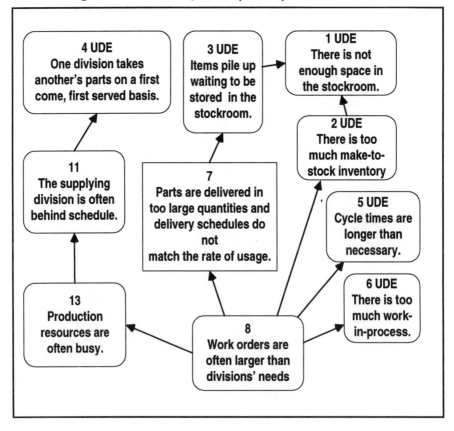

Exhibit A-8—Categories of Legitimate Reservations (reproduced with permission of the AGI)

A legitimate reservation exists when the logic presented does not make sense. The cause-effect relationship must always be stated as: IF C THEN E. There are two primary reasons for the observer to voice legitimate reservations when one presents a cause-effect relationship: ENTITY EXISTENCE and CAUSAL EXISTENCE. The observer can add to the explanation of his reservation by using 3 through 6 below to explain the specific nature of the reservation.

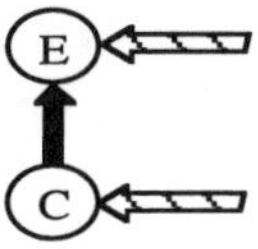

1. ENTITY EXISTENCE: Questioning the existence of the entity (cause or effect) by explaining that the cause or the effect does not actually exist.

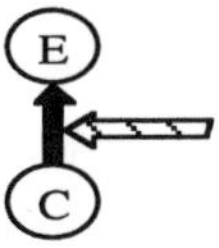

2. CAUSALITY EXISTENCE: Questioning the existence of the causal link between the cause and the effect by use of the IF ... THEN statement; by explaining that although we agree that both C and E exist, there is no direct link between the stated cause and the observed effect.

3. TAUTOLOGY: Being redundant in stating the cause-effect relationship. The cause is actually a rewording of the effect, thus being redundant. If a tautology exists, you can state the cause as being the effect and the effect as being the cause (e.g., the arrow could point in either direction). Therefore, the cause does not lead to the effect.

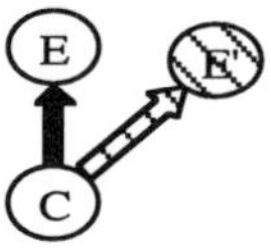

4. PREDICTED EFFECT (ENTITY) EXISTENCE: Using another effect (E') to show that the hypothesized cause (C) does not result in the initially observed effect (E). On the other hand, if the original cause also results in the additional effect, then this supports the original cause-effect relationship.

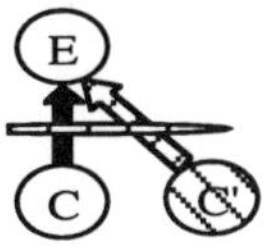

5. CAUSE INSUFFICIENCY: Explaining that an additional non-trivial cause must exist to explain the existence of the observed effect. If either of the hypothesized causes does not exist, then the observed effect will also not exist. IF C' AND IF C THEN E.

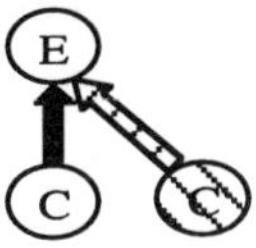

6. ADDITIONAL CAUSE: Explaining that an additional cause which adds to the size of the observed effect must exist. The causes magnify the size of the observed effect and neither cause by itself can totally explain the size or extent of the effect. The IF ... THEN statement is worded as follows: IF C' AND C, THEN E.

7. CLARITY: Not fully understanding the cause-effect relationship or the entity. Requesting an additional explanation of the cause-effect relationship or the entity.

LEGEND:  and  = original hypothesis.

 and 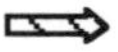 = legitimate reservations.

get at least some of the effect even if only one of the causes exists. In this case, the fact that there are often not enough parts available is not sufficient in itself (cause insufficiency) to get the effect that one division takes another's parts on a first-come, first-served basis. In addition, inventory must not have a divisional identity in order to get this effect. Therefore, a banana overlaps the arrows leading from entities 9 and 10 into entity 4. Note that because of a cause insufficiency challenge to the link between entities 13 and 11, entity 12 also was added to the tree.

Exhibit A-9
Constructing a Current Reality Tree (Part 5)

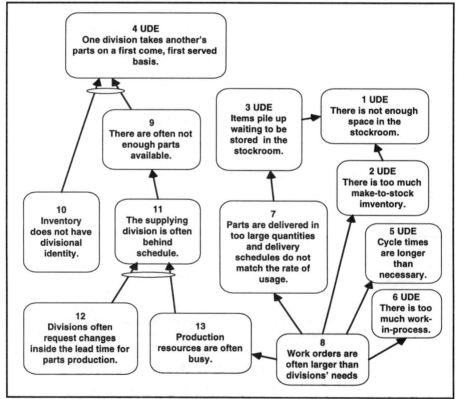

All of the original UDEs now have been linked, and the preparer is reasonably confident that the tree as a whole reflects his intuition. Most significantly, entity 8—"Work orders are often larger than divisions' needs"—has been identified as the core problem.

We will skip over Steps 6, 7, and 8 of the Guidelines for Building Current Reality Trees. Step 9 of the Guidelines advises the preparer to present the tree to someone else. Doing so helps to ensure that the tree does not have any gaping holes or logical errors. The other person reads the entire tree from the bottom up, one arrow at a time. Whenever an entity or an arrow is unclear or seems to be in error, the reader must use one of the Categories of Legitimate Reservations listed in Exhibit A-8. The reader is not allowed to say something such as "I don't buy it." The reservation must be specific and reasoned. Requiring the use of the Categories of Legitimate Reservations during such a review tends to defuse conflict and defensive posturing and keep discussion focused on the issues at hand. In addition, the Categories of Legitimate Reservations are an effective tool for equalizing influence in a group setting. Because all challenges to the tree must be framed using the Categories of Legitimate Reservations, it is difficult for one individual to dominate the process by force of personality or position. Subordinates can challenge their supervisor's tree more easily, and vice versa, without personalizing the criticism.

For example, the person who reviews the tree may feel that the links between entities 13, 11, and 4 are tenuous. However, the reviewer would have to be careful to phrase the objections in terms of the Categories of Legitimate Reservations. The reviewer might, for example, question whether the supplying division is in fact often behind schedule (entity 11), an entity existence reservation. The existence of the entity could be verified by reviewing the due dates on released work orders to determine if the supplying division is often behind schedule. Such rules for challenging trees may seem pedantic and confining, but we found at least one organization where the

Categories of Legitimate Reservations were not being used. The result was described as finger pointing and "politics as usual."

It is important to realize that trees ordinarily are not built starting with the core problem and working upwards. Rather, they are built starting with the Undesirable Effects and working downwards. While the core problem may not come as a big surprise to the preparer, usually the preparer would have had difficulty deducing the common cause by simply looking at the original list of Undesirable Effects. Put another way, building a Current Reality Tree is necessary when you are unable to deduce a common cause intuitively. It is also a good way to check intuition if you believe you already have figured out the core problem.

In summary the Current Reality Tree is used to deduce a common cause for the observable Undesirable Effects. If successful, it answers the question "What to change?" It does not, however, usually answer the questions "What to change to?" or "How to cause the change?" For example, the core problem in our example was identified as "work orders are often larger than divisions' needs." If it is really the core problem, the solution may seem trivial—just match the work orders to divisions' needs. However, three questions must be dealt with. First, if matching the work orders to divisions' needs is really a solution to the core problem, why hasn't it been implemented already? Second, what exactly will the new policy consist of? Third, how will we get people to accept the new policy? The remaining tools in the Thinking Process are designed to answer those questions.

Thinking Process—Evaporating Clouds

Goldratt states: "Our observation is that whenever a core problem is confronted, it turns out that the core problem was already intuitively very well known (even though not necessarily well verbalized) and already compromising solutions were implemented in a futile attempt to solve the problem. Inducing people to invent simple solutions requires that we steer them away from the avenues of compromise and towards the avenue of reexamining the foundations of the system, in order to find the minimum number of changes needed to create an environment in which the problem simply cannot exist."[2] Eliminating the core problem may not require compromise at all.

Why are core problems often associated with compromises? If a problem has an easy solution that does not involve any conflicts within the organization, then it is likely that the solution already will have been found and implemented. Therefore, if an easy solution has not already been implemented, it is likely there is some conflict in the organization that is blocking implementation. For example, conflicts often arise because of competing demands on resources. In such cases, the compromise solution is usually to give all of those who are competing for resources a "fair share" of the available resources. Unfortunately, such compromise solutions quite often are ineffective in dealing with the underlying core problem. Instead of acquiescing in compromise solutions that attempt to minimize conflict in the short term but are ultimately ineffective, Goldratt advocates eliminating the conditions that give rise to the conflict. He believes that all compromises require that both parties give up something, creating a "lose-lose" situation.

Situations involving conflicts are diagrammed in the Thinking Process as "Evaporating Clouds"—the general form of which is displayed in Exhibit A-10. The objective of the cloud (which could be the elimination of the core problem) is the desired outcome. The objective A has two requirements, B and C. That is, in order to have the objective A, apparently you must first have the requirements B and C. In the standard Evaporating Cloud presentation, each of these requirements has a prerequisite. To have the requirement B, you apparently must have the prerequisite D. But in order to have the requirement C, you also must apparently have the prerequisite Not D. The conflict occurs because you cannot have both D and Not D si-

Exhibit A-10
Generic Evaporating Cloud

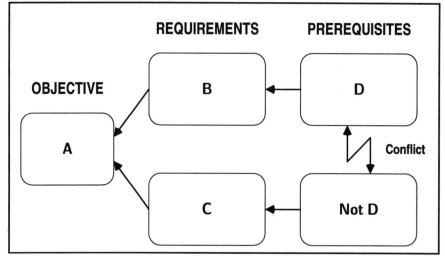

multaneously, and therefore it appears that the objective is unobtainable.

For example, suppose the core problem is "our compensation scheme does not motivate salespersons to increase the company's profit." In that case, the objective is simply the opposite of the core problem or "our compensation scheme *does* motivate salespersons to increase the company's profit." While this is the objective, it is not an implementable solution. Moreover, there is usually some reason why the objective that would eliminate the core problem has not been achieved already. In this example, there is probably some reason—most likely a conflict—why the company's compensation scheme does not motivate salespersons to increase the company's profit.

To make this idea concrete, refer to Exhibit A-11, which illustrates an Evaporating Cloud associated with the objective "our compensation scheme motivates salespersons to increase the company's profit." This Evaporating Cloud should be read as follows: To have a compensation scheme that motivates salespersons to increase the company's profit (Objective A), salespersons must feel that their performance measure fairly reflects their own efforts (Requirement B).[3] And to have a compensation scheme that motivates salespersons to increase the company's profit (Objective A), compensation must be tied to the salesperson's contribution to company profits (Objective C). These two necessary conditions must be fulfilled at the same time to have Objective A.

The problem is that salespersons will feel that the performance measure fairly reflects their own efforts (Requirement B) only if their compensation is tied just to elements that they can control (Prerequisite D), but to tie salespersons' contribution to company profits (Requirement C), apparently compensation *must* be tied to elements

Exhibit A-11
Example of an Evaporating Cloud

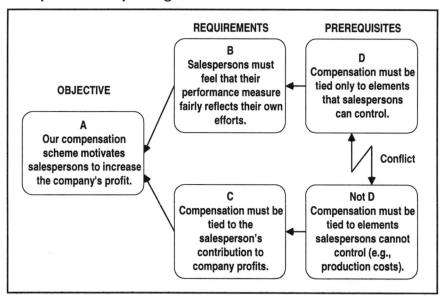

such as production costs that the salespersons cannot control (Prerequisite Not D). It appears that the prerequisites to the necessary conditions are in direct conflict. To obtain the objective we must satisfy the necessary conditions, but apparently they cannot be satisfied unless the salesperson's compensation is both tied to and not tied to the same thing.

The usual compromise solution is to make salespersons responsible for those elements of profit that they obviously can control to some extent—namely, sales. This is a compromise because it does tie compensation to an element over which the salespersons feel they have some control, and it is an element that does impact profits. However, as with most compromise solutions, it does not really achieve the objective. While tying compensation to sales does motivate salespersons to increase the company's sales, it does not motivate them to increase the company's profit. The difference between the two objectives is clear when it comes to setting prices and discounts. Decreasing a price almost always will result in greater total sales.[4] Because lower prices almost always will result in greater total sales, salespersons who are compensated on the basis of sales alone inevitably will want to cut prices.

Because compromise solutions are usually ineffective, one might jump to the conclusion that the manager in this situation should just "bite the bullet" and choose one of the requirements and give up on the other one. That is, the manager should take the plunge and tie compensation directly to the salespersons' contribution to company profits. However, if both A and B are truly requirements for the objective, this solution will not work. If compensation is tied to the salespersons' contribution to company profits (rather than to their sales), but they do not feel that their performance is being measured fairly, then the compensation scheme will not motivate them properly to increase the company's profit. Instead of going for a lopsided or compromise solution, Goldratt advocates eliminating the conditions under which the conflict occurs:

The Evaporating Clouds method does not strive to reach a compromise solution, rather it concentrates on invalidating the problem itself. The first attack is made on the objective itself asking, 'Do we really want it?'. . . . [L]et's assume for now that the objective has been checked and verified. Yes, we do want to achieve this specific objective. Is the only way open to turn to the avenue of compromise? The answer is definitely not. What we have to remind ourselves of, is that the arrows in the Evaporating Clouds diagram, the arrows connecting the requirements to the objective, the prerequisite to the requirements and the arrow of conflict, all these arrows are just logical connections. One of the most basic fundamentals of logic is that behind any logical connection there is an assumption. In our case, most probably it is a hidden assumption. . . . The Evaporating Clouds technique is based on verbalizing the assumptions hidden behind the arrows, forcing them out and challenging them. It's enough to invalidate even one of these assumptions, no matter which one, and the problem collapses, disappears.[5]

Essentially, evaporating the cloud consists of exposing an invalid assumption underlying one of the arrows. A solution that breaks one of the arrows in the Evaporating Cloud is called an "injection." The process of identifying the particular underlying assumption that should be challenged is subject to its own set of guidelines. We will not go into the details. In the example illustrated in Exhibit A-11, the most vulnerable arrow in the Evaporating Cloud diagram is probably the one connecting Not D to C. The hidden assumption is that salespersons' contributions to the company's profits cannot be measured without holding them responsible for elements (such as production costs) that are beyond their control. However, this underlying assumption is false. It is possible to do a much better job of measuring salespersons' contribution to profit than using just sales—and without holding him or her responsible for anything more than selling prices and sales volume. This task can be accomplished by mea-

Exhibit A-12
The Evaporating Cloud for the Core Problem in Exhibit A-9

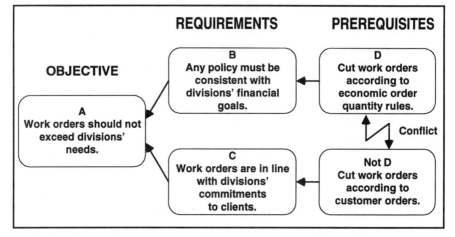

suring the salesperson's performance by the total contribution margin (in Goldratt's terms, the throughput) that he or she generates. To insulate salespersons from elements they cannot control, all nonselling costs deducted in the contribution margin computation can be standard variable costs.

Note that as a result of examining the Evaporating Cloud, the solution itself has been refined. "Tie salespersons' compensation to their total contribution margin at standard cost" is a more specific solution than "motivate salespersons to increase the company's profit."[6]

To reinforce the notion of the Evaporating Cloud, return to the Current Reality Tree in Exhibit A-9. The core problem at the bottom of the tree is "work orders are often larger than divisions' needs." The solution seems obvious—match work orders to the divisions' real needs. However, there is probably a reason why this obvious solution has not been implemented already. The cloud underlying this core problem is illustrated in Exhibit A-12.

This particular cloud can be evaporated by exposing the assumptions underlying the arrow connecting B and D. The B-D connection states that it is necessary to cut work orders according to economic order quantities to meet divisions' financial goals. The underlying assumption is that real costs are involved in setting up batches. Typically, batch setup costs are overestimated by cost accounting systems at the nonconstraints and grossly underestimated at the constraint. Setup time is basically free at the nonconstraints, and the only real costs are supplies and first-past rejects. When it is realized that batch setups are far less costly than usually assumed, the apparent conflict between D and not D evaporates. If batch setups are basically free, the typical customer order will be larger than the minimum batch size.

The Future Reality Tree

We will not go into any detail concerning the remaining elements of the Thinking Process—the Future Reality Tree, the Prerequisite Tree, and the Transition Tree. However, we will use a simple example to give some idea of what these techniques are all about. We apologize if the example seems too frivolous, but we need a very simple and familiar situation to explain these techniques expeditiously.

The example is the Old Testament story that forms the basis for King Solomon's reputation for wisdom.[7] Two women living in the same house each had a baby boy within a few days of each other. Shortly thereafter, one of the babies died in the night and both women claimed the surviving baby as their own. There were no witnesses to corroborate either woman's claim and the problem seemed intractable, so the dispute was brought to Solomon for a judgment. Solomon might have drawn up the Current Reality Tree that appears in Exhibit A-13.

In this case, the Current Reality Tree doesn't yield any insights. The core problem—"I can't figure out a just resolution to this dispute"—is fairly obvious without constructing the Current Reality

Tree. It is normally worthwhile to construct a Current Reality Tree only when the core problem is not apparent and the preparer feels that he or she is foundering. In Goldratt's words, "The preparer should construct a Current Reality Tree when he has the feeling that he is in a swimming pool full of ping-pong balls (UDEs) and he is unsuccessfully trying to hold them all under water at the same time." Solomon might have jumped right to the Evaporating Cloud without bothering with the Current Reality Tree. The objective of the Evaporating Cloud is the opposite of the core problem. In this case, the objective would be "come to a just resolution of the dispute." The

Exhibit A-13
Solomon's Current Reality Tree

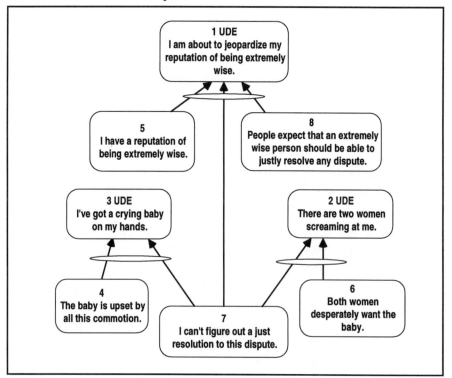

Exhibit A-14
Solomon's Evaporating Cloud

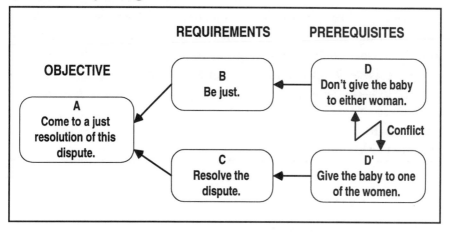

Evaporating Cloud might appear as in Exhibit A-14.

Solomon's problem is that he is being pulled between giving the baby to one of the women in order to get the dispute out of the way and his desire on the other hand to be just, which demands that he not give the baby to the wrong woman. The particular hidden assumption he attacked is the one between D and B. The connection is read as follows: "To be just, I must not give the baby to either woman." However, with the addition of the hidden assumption, the connection is read as "to be just, I must not give the baby to either woman because the existing evidence is insufficient to determine who the real mother is." Solomon's injection, which would invalidate the hidden assumption and break the arrow between D and B is "the real mother will reveal herself to me."

From this point onward, we embellish the basic Biblical story somewhat for the purpose of illustrating the use of the Thinking Process. At least by reputation, Solomon had powerful intuition that could lead him directly to a superior solution. However, those of us blessed with less insight might need some help. For purposes of illustration, let us suppose that Solomon proceeded to solve his problem using the Thinking Process. The next step would be to build a Future Reality Tree in which the injection will lead, we hope, to the opposites of the original Undesirable Effects. The first attempt at such a Future Reality Tree appears in Exhibit A-15. A Future Reality Tree is very similar to a Current Reality Tree, except that the injections—the actions to be taken as part of the solution—are en-

Exhibit A-15
Solomon's First Future Reality Tree

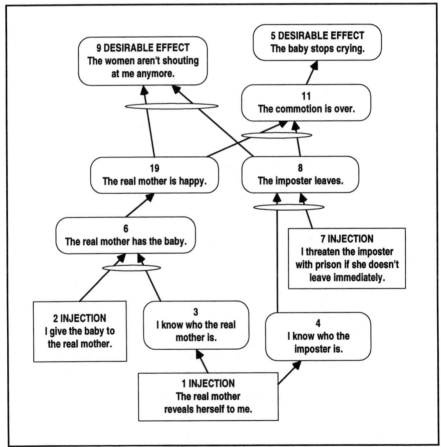

closed in squared-off boxes. In the process of building the Future Reality Tree, additional injections often are added to develop the solution and to head off possible negative consequences. In this case, the obvious additional injection (entity 2) of actually giving the baby to the real mother has been added at the bottom of the tree. In addition, the injection "threaten the woman who lied with prison" stops her shouting.

According to the Future Reality Tree, the solution is moving along smoothly; however, at this point it is not at all clear how to implement the injection "the real mother reveals herself to me." This kind of an injection is called a "flying pig" because it seems to rely on a miracle. Moreover, the injections do not necessarily eliminate *all* of the Undesirable Effects. If the real mother reveals herself spontaneously without any apparent action taken by Solomon to induce this revelation, Solomon's reputation for wisdom is still in danger. He must take some action in order to preserve and enhance his reputation. This realization leads to the refinement of the Future Reality Tree shown in Exhibit A-16. Note that the injections now eliminate all of the Undesirable Effects.

At this stage, the injection, albeit refined, still looks like a "flying pig." In order to trim its wings, the "negative branch reservation" is used. In other words, we try to verbalize what makes the injection unreal—what the difficulty is. In our case, it is obvious that there is at least one potential problem with implementing the injection at the bottom of the refined Future Reality Tree in Exhibit A-16. The imposter undoubtedly will attempt to mimic the reactions of a real mother—making it difficult to create a situation in which the real mother will reveal herself. This particular negative branch reservation is displayed in Exhibit A-17 as a partial tree. If the imposter successfully imitates the behavior of a real mother, then Solomon will not be able to tell who the real mother is and all of the Undesirable Effects will remain. The key in such a situation is to surface an assumption underlying an arrow that leads to the negative conclusion. In this case, the arrow connecting entities 20 and 21 assumes the imposter will mimic the behavior of the mother in every situation. Solomon's solution, therefore, must create a specific situation in which the imposter will not mimic the real mother's behavior.

Exhibit A-16
Solomon's Second Future Reality Tree

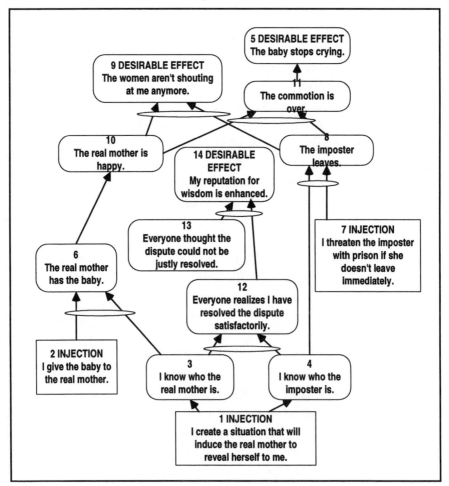

The critical question of *how* Solomon is going to create such a situation remains. Simply verbalizing the requirements and putting everything down on paper can contribute enormously to the creative process. Nevertheless, we suspect that just plain ingenuity—if not divine inspiration—may sometimes be required. The Thinking Process may not be enough. At any rate, let us suppose that Solomon was able to hit upon the idea of cutting the baby in half to induce different reactions in the two women. This injection is used to flesh out his Future Reality Tree in Exhibit A-18.

Now Solomon is ready for the next step in the Thinking Process—the Prerequisite Tree.

Exhibit A-17
Solomon's Negative Branch Reservation

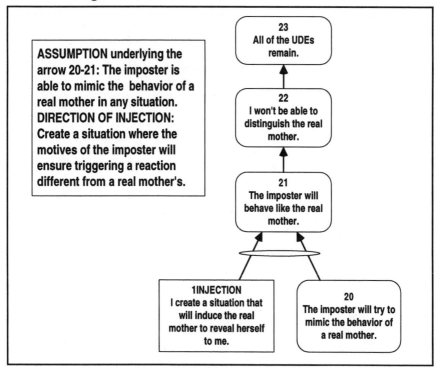

Exhibit A-18
Solomon's Final Future Reality Tree

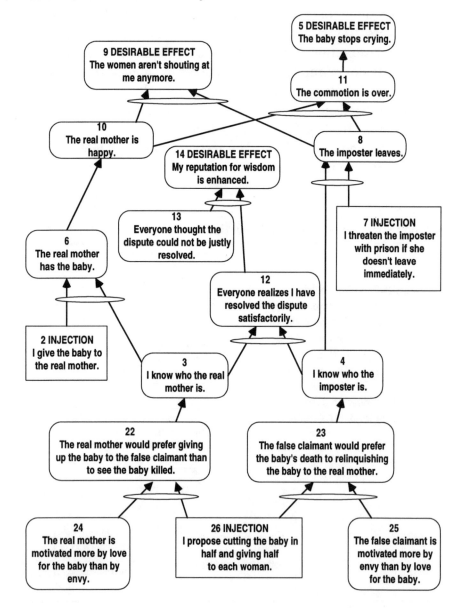

The Prerequisite Tree

The purpose of the Prerequisite Tree is to identify obstacles to implementation. The Transition Tree, which comes later, deals with the obstacles identified in the Prerequisite Tree. To begin the Prerequisite Tree, one of the injections is placed at the top. In this case, the injection "the real mother reveals herself to me when I threaten to give half of the baby to each woman" is the starting point. Solomon's Prerequisite Tree appears in Exhibit A-19. In this case, the obstacle that "The false claimant may take compassion and relent first" is listed as entity 2 in the Prerequisite Tree. When an obstacle is identified, the preparer should write down an "intermediate objective" that would overcome the obstacle. If a specific action does not immediately pop into mind, the intermediate objective is written as simply the opposite of the obstacle. In this case, Solomon defines the intermediate objective to be "the false claimant will not relent first." If this intermediate objective is achieved, then the obstacle will be overcome and the objective at the top of the tree achieved. Because the objective at the top of the tree is the injection required to eliminate all of the Undesirable Effects, achieving the intermediate objective will result in solving the problem.

The use of the arrows in the Prerequisite Tree may be confusing. These arrows have a different meaning from the arrows in the other trees. The connections among three entities in Exhibit A-19 should be read in the following way: to have the objective "the real mother reveals herself to me when I threaten to give half of the baby to each woman," we must have the intermediate objective "the false claimant will not relent first" because of the obstacle "the false claimant may take compassion and relent first."

The ordering of the intermediate objectives in the Prerequisite Tree is significant. There is an implicit time dependency in the Prerequisite Tree so that the intermediate objectives should be achieved in reverse order, starting from the bottom of the tree.

Exhibit A-19
Solomon's Prerequisite Tree

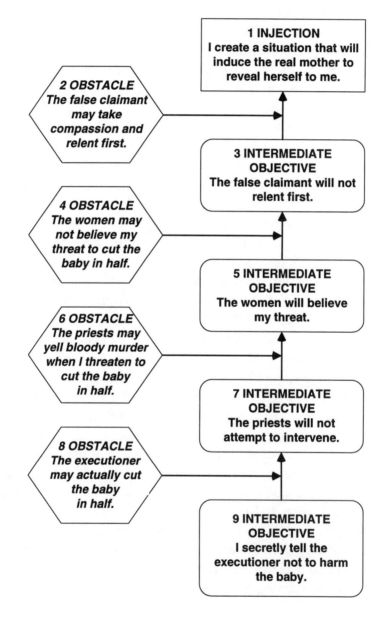

The next step is the construction of a Transition Tree, which provides the details of how the intermediate objectives will be attained and hence the obstacles overcome.

The Transition Tree

The Transition Tree is the action plan. All of the intermediate objectives should occur as consequences of specific actions in the Transition Tree. The implementation plan, as revealed in the Transition Tree in Exhibit A-20, is slightly more involved than Solomon's action in the biblical story. A monetary sweetener has been added that should make the false claimant even more likely to react differently than the real mother. In addition, a bit of theatrical sword-sharpening has been added to make the threat more convincing, and the priests have been dismissed to forestall their interference. These may seem like rather silly additions to the Biblical story, but they illustrate a potentially important point. Managers we interviewed said that the process of building Prerequisite and Transition Trees results in more robust solutions than casually laid plans do and that the solutions are more likely to result in the desired outcomes. The Prerequisite Tree forces one to think about the obstacles likely to crop up, and the Transition Tree forces one to deal with them systematically.

There is another advantage to using the Thinking Process. In the original biblical story, Solomon quickly arrived at a solution using just his innate reasoning abilities and his intuition. However, those in the court who heard his order, "Cut the baby in half and give half to each mother," undoubtedly were horrified and would have intervened if they could. Solomon was able to pull it off because of his authority. Those of us who are not blessed with such authority may have to rely more on persuasion to enlist support for our plans. A number of managers told us that the trees are great devices for quickly communicating plans and the reasons for the plans and often

Exhibit A-20
Solomon's Transition Tree

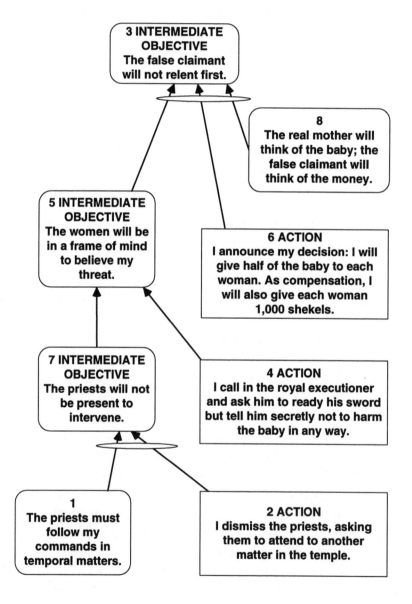

help build consensus by making the change process more transparent and understandable.

The danger we face in using this Old Testament story to illustrate the Thinking Process is that it may seem like an awful lot of work for such a simple situation. It is. The cost/benefit trade-offs become more favorable for the use of the Thinking Process as the problems become more complex and therefore more difficult to grasp on a strictly intuitive level. We have included some examples of the use of the Thinking Process in Chapter 3 where the problems are a bit more complex.

Summary of the Thinking Process

As an aid in summarizing the Thinking Process, we have reproduced in Exhibit A-21 an overview prepared by the AGI. As we have discussed, the Current Reality Tree is used to identify a core problem, typically one of the entry points near the bottom of the tree. Once the core problem has been identified, the objective is the opposite of the core problem. Unfortunately, an existing conflict in the current reality often prevents the organization from attaining the objective easily. The Evaporating Cloud is used to identify an injection that changes the current reality so that the conflict disappears.

To check this solution, a Future Reality Tree is constructed from the bottom up, starting with the injection. If the injection is effective, it will result in an environment in which the Undesirable Effects have disappeared and have been replaced by their opposites—Desirable Effects. Usually the original injection is not sufficient, and additional injections must be added to the tree. An important part of the process of building the Future Reality Tree is to check for new Undesirable Effects that might result from the injections.

The Future Reality Tree provides some assurance that if the injections are implemented, the desired outcomes will be realized. However, it would be rash to rush into implementation. Instead, it is usu-

Exhibit A-21
Overview of the Thinking Process

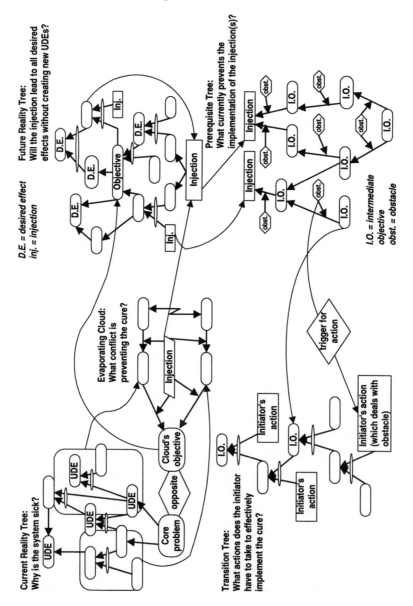

ally a good idea to break the implementation plan down into a series of small steps. This process is carried out with the Prerequisite Tree, which starts with the desired injections at the top. All of the imaginable obstacles to implementation are included on the tree. Each obstacle gives rise to an intermediate objective, which should be sufficient to overcome the obstacle. In the completed Prerequisite Tree the intermediate objectives should be sequenced from bottom to top of the tree in the order in which they should be accomplished.

The Transition Tree provides the actual implementation plan— the actions that should be taken to achieve the ultimate objectives. The actions achieve the intermediate objectives as detailed in the Transition Tree. If the intermediate objectives are achieved, the obstacles will be overcome and the injections will be achieved as detailed in the Prerequisite Tree. If the injections are achieved, then the desired outcomes will be achieved as detailed in the Future Reality Tree. The implementation plan in the Transition Tree provides a safety net of sorts because it involves a sequence of small steps with reality checks along the way. If reality does not unfold as predicted, the process can be stopped and the plan modified.

This discussion of the Thinking Process may be a bit misleading in that it seems to imply that every problem must be analyzed using all of the Thinking Process from the Current Reality Tree all the way to the Transition Tree. This is not true. In fact, the AGI recommends the use of isolated elements of the Thinking Process to deal with particular problems. If all you want to do is isolate a root cause, use the Current Reality Tree. Once the core problem has been identified, the entire solution may be entirely transparent. The Evaporating Cloud technique might be used to expose and resolve a conflict in negotiations. A Transition Tree might be used to structure a business plan. All of these isolated uses of the Thinking Process are legitimate; however, the entire process is available if there is a need to go all the way from diagnosis of the problem through a specific implementation plan.

Notes

1. The Thinking Process requires new ways of thinking, uses unfamiliar terms, and is complex, which poses a challenge for us as the authors of this book. To convey some sense of the mechanics of the Thinking Process, our examples should be simple. On the other hand, if the examples are simple, it may not be clear why the Thinking Process is necessary. The power of the Thinking Process is most evident in cases where the problem is complex and solutions are not intuitively obvious. We have chosen to use simple examples but realize that some readers may underestimate the potential value of the tools because of the simplicity of the examples.

2. Eliyahu M. Goldratt, *The Theory of Constraints*, North River Press, Croton-on-Hudson, N.Y., 1990, pp. 36-37.

3. The direction of the arrows in the Evaporating Cloud may seem confusing to some readers; the arrows have different meanings in the Current Reality Tree and in the Evaporating Cloud diagrams. In the Current Reality Tree, the arrows indicate "sufficiency" whereas the arrows in the Evaporating Cloud indicate "necessity." In the Current Reality Tree, the arrows are read "if you have the entity at the source of the arrow, then you have the entity at the end of the arrow." In the Evaporating Cloud, the arrows are read "to have the entity at the end of the arrow, you must have the entity at the source of the arrow." This may seem like splitting hairs, but there is a very significant difference between sufficient conditions on the one hand and necessary conditions on the other. Take, for example, the statement "If I give the keys to the car to my daughter, then she can go driving." She also could get the keys from her mother, so that my giving her the keys would be sufficient, but not necessary, for her to go driving. In contrast, consider the statement "For my daughter to go driving, she must have the keys to the car." In this case, having the keys to the car is a necessary condition for her to drive the car. (You may object that she might be able to go driving without the keys—she could hot-wire the car instead. This is, in fact, an example of what Goldratt means when he suggests we should examine the assumptions underlying the arrows. We may be able to break an arrow by exposing an unstated assumption. In this case, the unstated assumption is that there is no way to go driving without the keys to the car.)

4. Consider the profit possibilities in a market in which the opposite is true—increasing prices results in greater total sales. In such a market, increasing prices would result in greater revenue and in lower costs because of the lower volume that comes with higher prices. The profit possibilities would be boundless.

5. Goldratt, op. cit., pp. 44, 47-48.

6. This solution to motivating salespersons more appropriately is well known and is discussed in many management accounting texts. Because it is such a well-known solution, it is likely that there is some reason why it has not been widely adopted. In other words, there is probably some conflict over the use of the total contribution margin as a means of evaluating salesmen that could be analyzed with yet another Evaporating Cloud.

7. 1 Kings 3: 16-28.

Institute of Management Accountants
Committee on Research
1992-93

Dennis L. Neider, CMA
Chairman
Price Waterhouse
New York, New York

Jack C. Bailes
Oregon State University
Corvallis, Oregon

Frederick M. Cole
University of North Florida
Jacksonville, Florida

James P. Conley
Ernst & Young
Atlanta, Georgia

Paul P. Danesi, Jr.
Worldwide Products
Texas Instruments, Inc.
Attleboro, Massachusetts

David W. Goodrich
Columbia Gas System, Inc.
Wilmington, Delaware

John Karabec
IBM Corporation
Tarrytown, New York

David R. Koeppen
Boise State University
Boise, Idaho

Charles D. Mecimore
University of North Carolina
Greensboro, North Carolina

Robert J. Melby
Defense Contract Audit Agency
Memphis, Tennessee

Robert C. Miller
The Boeing Company
Seattle, Washington

Wayne J. Morse
Clarkson University
Potsdam, New York

Linda M. Onis
Citibank, N.A.
Long Island City, New York

Grover L. Porter
University of Alabama
Huntsville, Alabama

W. Ron Ragland
Martin Marietta Energy Systems, Inc.
Oak Ridge, Tennessee

Michael Robinson
Baylor University
Waco, Texas

Harold P. Roth, CMA
University of Tennessee
Knoxville, Tennessee

Arjan T. Sadhwani
University of Akron
Akron, Ohio

Lloyd O. Schatschneider
Lerner Publications Co.
Minneapolis, Minnesota

Charles J. Smith, Jr.
Gruner & Jahr USA Group, Inc.
New York, New York

Richard B. Troxel, CMA
Capital Accounting
Washington, D.C.

Ray Vander Weele, CMA
Office of Pensions & Insurance
Grand Rapids, Michigan

Robert C. Young
Digital Equipment Corp.
Nashua, New Hampshire